Additional Praise for *A Dash of Style*

"[Noah Lukeman] provides incredible insight for those individuals endeavoring to entertain and inspire future generations with their words." —Amazon.com editorial team
(referring to an Amazon shorts excerpt of *A Dash of Style*)

"Lukeman makes a case for punctuation as being instrumental in revealing the soul of a writer; he compares punctuation to musical composition, and sees the combination of commas, colons, semicolons, dashes, ellipses, question marks, italics, hyphens, quotation marks, and full stops as a writer's version of a symphony. What keeps *A Dash of Style* enjoyable are the examples Lukeman selects to illustrate his points. We get to compare and contrast the illuminating styles of writers as diverse as Hemingway, Kafka, Joyce, Shakespeare, Melville, Faulkner, Poe, Forster, Lessing, Crane, Carver, Elizabeth Barrett Browning, and T. S. Eliot. Lukeman allows us to consider punctuation as a prelude to great writing. Certainly worthy of an exclamation point. Or two!!" —Lawrence Grobel, lecturer on interviewing and the literature of journalism at UCLA, and *New York Times* best-selling author of *The Art of the Interview, The Hustons,* and *Al Pacino*

"I thought I knew everything there is to know about teaching punctuation. Lukeman's *A Dash of Style* taught me otherwise. Whether one wishes to write fiction, poetry, drama, screenplays, or just great English, Lukeman's third book masterfully unveils how punctuation affects the minds and emotions of readers. *A Dash of Style* needs to be on every aspiring and accomplished author's work desk!" —Dr. Ervin Nieves, Department of English, Clarke College, Dubuque, Iowa

"I found *A Dash of Style* to be as clear and beautifully written as Lukeman's first two books. Once again, he has composed a text that is perfectly organized, conveys important but subtle truths, and is unique in perspective. I will recommend the book to my students and perhaps give it as a gift to friends who write. A punctuation book for the creative writer. What a great idea."

—Laura Oliver,
adjunct English faculty, University of Maryland

"Lukeman has answered my unuttered cry for a punctuation guide for creative writers. In fact, I hadn't realized that I needed it until now. My students fail to understand the need for punctuation, and I have relied on grammar books from English composition— painfully inadequate and misleading for fiction. *A Dash of Style* is a delightful shift. I see genius at work here."

—Dr. Peggy Brown, professor,
Collin County Community College, Georgia

"Here's a book that offers not only the mechanics of punctuation but also the means to make your writing soar."

—Alexander Steele, dean of faculty,
Gotham Writers' Workshop

"I've never seen punctuation elucidated in such a directly helpful manner. All creative writers, from the just-starting-out to the most stylistically sophisticated, will benefit from Lukeman's savvy advice."

—Therese Eiben, former editor of
Poets & Writers and editor of
The Practical Writer

A DASH OF STYLE

ALSO BY NOAH LUKEMAN

The First Five Pages

The Plot Thickens

A

DASH

OF

STYLE

The Art and Mastery

of Punctuation

N O A H   L U K E M A N

W. W. Norton & Company

New York   London

For information about permission to reproduce selections from this book, write to
Permissions, W. W. Norton & Company, Inc., 500 Fifth Avenue, New York, NY 10110

Manufacturing by Quebecor Fairfield
Book design by Joanne Metsch
Production manager: Julia Druskin

Library of Congress Cataloging-in-Publication Data

Lukeman, Noah.
A dash of style : the art and mastery of punctuation / Noah Lukeman. —
1st ed.
p. cm.
Includes bibliographical references.
ISBN-13: 978-0-393-06087-X (hardcover)
ISBN-10: 0-393-06087-X (hardcover)
1. English language–Punctuation. I. Title.
PE1450.L85 2006

2005031827

W. W. Norton & Company, Inc., 500 Fifth Avenue, New York, N.Y. 10110
www.wwnorton.com

W. W. Norton & Company Ltd., Castle House, 75/76 Wells Street, London W1T 3QT

1 2 3 4 5 6 7 8 9 0

For my father

Of all the subjects which engage the attention of the compositor, none proves a greater stumbling-block, or is so much a matter of uncertainty and doubt . . . as the Art of Punctuation.

—Henry Beadnell,

Spelling and Punctuation, 1880

CONTENTS

Acknowledgments / 11
Introduction / 13

Part 1 | THE TRIUMVIRATE / 17

Chapter 1: The Period (the Stop Sign) / 21
Chapter 2: The Comma (the Speed Bump) / 44
Chapter 3: The Semicolon (the Bridge) / 69

Part 2 | INTO THE LIMELIGHT / 87

Chapter 4: The Colon (the Magician) / 91
Chapter 5: The Dash and Parentheses
   (the Interrupter and the Advisor) / 111
Chapter 6: Quotation Marks (the Trumpets) / 139
Chapter 7: The Paragraph and Section Breaks
   (the Stoplight and the Town Line) / 159

Part 3 | PROCEED WITH CAUTION / 181

Chapter 8: The Question Mark, Exclamation Point,
   Italics, Points of Ellipsis, and the Hyphen / 183

Epilogue: The Symphony of Punctuation / 192

Suggested Reading / 203

ACKNOWLEDGMENTS

I would like to thank Jill Bialosky for her editorial passion for the book, and for her poet's eye in the revision process. I would like to thank her editorial assistant, Evan Carver, who brought a great deal of enthusiasm, and offered fine suggestions. I would like to thank the entire Norton editorial team, who have been behind this book from the beginning and lent it great support throughout.

I would like to thank my copyeditor, David Stanford Burr. It was an honor to have this book copyedited by a member of the Advisory Board of *The Chicago Manual of Style*, fifteenth edition, and it was certainly the most brilliant copyedit I have yet received.

At Norton, I would like to thank the managing editor, Nancy Palmquist; my publicist, Winfrida Mbewe; my project editor, Don Rifkin; my art director, Gina Webster; and the associate director of subsidiary rights, Felice Mello.

In the UK, I am grateful to Caspain Dennis, Tessa Ingham, and the Abner Stein Agency for their steadfast support, and to Judy Pearsall, Rachel De Wachter, and Ben Harris at Oxford University Press. In Spain, I am grateful to Montse Yanez and Sandra Biel for their efforts.

I am grateful to Kristin Godsey and the entire *Writers Digest* family, and to Elfreida Abbe at *The Writer* and Supriya Bhatnagar at the *AWP Chronicle* for their early support.

I am grateful to the many professors and writers who contributed their thoughts on punctuation. Among them are Ellen Cooney, John Smolens, Paul Cody, Phyllis Moore, Joe Jackson, Kent Meyers, and Daniel Myerson.

And as always, I am deeply grateful to my family for all of their love and support.

INTRODUCTION

Intellectually, stops matter a great deal. If you are getting your commas, semicolons, and full stops wrong, it means that you are not getting your thoughts right, and your mind is muddled.
    —WILLIAM TEMPLE, Archbishop of York,
        as reported in *The Observer*, 1938

THIS IS not a book for grammarians. Nor is it one for historians. They can turn to Lynne Truss's *Eats, Shoots & Leaves* or a host of other excellent punctuation books written for them. This book is for the audience that needs it the most and yet for whom, ironically, a punctuation book has yet to be written: creative writers. This means writers of fiction, nonfiction, memoir, poetry, and screenplays, and also includes anyone seeking to write well, whether for business, school, or any other endeavor.

I believe most writers do not want to know the seventeen uses of the comma, or ponder the fourth-century usage of the semicolon. Most writers simply want to improve their writing. They want to know how punctuation can serve *them*—not how they can serve punctuation. They have turned to books on punctuation, but have found most painfully mundane. Unfortunately, many of these books tend to ignore anyone hoping to use punctuation with a bit of style.

This book will offer a fresh look at punctuation: as an art form. Punctuation is often discussed as a convenience, as a way of facilitating what you want to say. Rarely is it pondered as a medium for artistic expression, as a means of impacting the content—not in a pedantic way, but in the most profound way, where it achieves symbiosis with the narration, style, viewpoint, and even the plot itself.

Why did Hemingway lean heavily on the period? Why did Faulkner eschew it? Why did Poe and Melville rely on the semi-colon? Why did Dickinson embrace the dash, Stein avoid the comma? How could the punctuation differ so radically between these great authors? What did punctuation add that language itself could not?

There is an underlying rhythm to all text. Sentences crash and fall like the waves of the sea, and work unconsciously on the reader. Punctuation is the music of language. As a conductor can influence the experience of a song by manipulating its rhythm, so can punctuation influence the reading experience, bring out the best (or worst) in a text. By controlling the speed of a text, punctuation dictates how it should be read.

A delicate world of punctuation lives just beneath the surface of your work, like a world of microorganisms living in a pond. They are missed by the naked eye, but if you use a microscope you'll find they exist, and that the pond is, in fact, teeming with life. This book will teach you to become sensitive to this habitat. The more you do, the greater the likelihood of your crafting a finer work in every respect. Conversely, the more you turn a blind eye, the greater the likelihood of your creating a cacophonous text, and of your being misread.

This book is interactive. It will ask you to make punctuation your own, to grapple with it by way of numerous exercises in a way you haven't before. You'll discover that working with punctuation will actually spark new ideas for your writing. Writing a new work (or revising an old one) with a fresh approach to punctuation opens a world of possibilities, enables you to write and think in a way you haven't before. Ultimately, you'll find this book is not about making you a better grammarian, but about making you a better writer.

Along these lines, I will not exhaustively catalog every punctuation mark, nor will I examine every usage of every mark discussed. Apostrophes and slashes can be left to grammarians. What interests me are the most important uses of the most important marks, those that can impact a text creatively. I am not concerned here whether an apostrophe goes before or after an "s," or whether a colon precedes a list; I am concerned, rather, whether adding or subtracting a dash will alter the intention of a scene.

The benefits of punctuation for the creative writer are limitless, if you know how to tap them. You can, for example, create a stream-of-consciousness effect using periods; indicate a passing of time using commas; add complexity using parentheses; capture a certain form of dialogue using dashes; build to a revelation using colons; increase your pace using paragraph breaks; keep readers hooked using section breaks. This—its impact on content—is the holy grail of punctuation, too often buried in long discussions of grammar and history.

As a literary agent I've read tens of thousands of manuscripts, and I've come to learn that punctuation, more than anything, belies clarity —or chaos—of thought. Flaws in the writing can be spotted most quickly by the punctuation, while strengths extolled by the same medium. Punctuation reveals the writer. Ultimately, the end result of any work is only as good as the method in getting there, and there is no way there without these strange dots and lines and curves we call punctuation.

Part 1

THE TRIUMVIRATE

(the period, comma, and semicolon)

Punctuation in skilled hands is a remarkably subtle system of signals, signs, symbols and winks that keep readers on the smoothest road. Too subtle, perhaps: Has any critic or reviewer ever praised an author for being a master of punctuation, a virtuoso of commas? Has anyone ever won a Pulitzer, much less a Nobel, for elegant distinctions between dash and colon, semicolon and comma?

—RENE J. CAPPON,
The Associated Press Guide to Punctuation

Let's begin by looking at the three crucial punctuation marks—the period, comma, and semicolon—primarily responsible for sentence construction. They can make or break sentences and, as such, have supreme power. Indeed, with these three marks alone you can effectively punctuate a book. It might not be as subtle or complex as a work that contains the additional marks covered in part 2, but it would be perfectly functional. In fact, great authors have punctuated works employing even fewer than these three marks.

As you'll see, these marks sometimes divide, other times connect, yet always they wield power over structure. The period would be impossibly far away if it weren't for the comma and semicolon, which allow a much-needed pause. The comma would be stuck in endless pauses if it weren't for the period to teach it how to stop; and the gracious semicolon wouldn't exist if it weren't for the failure of both the comma and period to fulfill its task.

Consequently, in part 1 we will consider these three marks together: as a triumvirate.

THE PERIOD

(the Stop Sign)

No iron can stab the heart with such a force as a period put just at the right place.

—Isaac Babel,
"Guy de Maupassant"

The period is the stop sign of the punctuation world. By providing a boundary, a period delineates a thought. Its presence divides and its absence connects. To employ it is to make a statement; to leave it out, equally so. All other punctuation marks exist only to modify what lies between two periods—they are always restrained by it, and must act in context of it. To realize its power, simply imagine a book without any periods. Or one with a period after every word. Consequently, the period also sets the tone for style and pacing.

HOW TO USE IT

Some authors, like Camus, Carver, and Hemingway, used the period heavily. Although short sentences tend to be dismissed as amateur or juvenile, there are times when short sentences work well, when a work can even demand such a style. In some instances, to achieve a certain effect, it is more natural for a period to be used heavily. Here are a few:

• The beginning or ending of a chapter or book. A short sentence can be used to hook a reader and to add a heightened sense of drama. Consider the opening of Ray Bradbury's novel *Fahrenheit 451*:

> It was a pleasure to burn.

Or of Patrick Quinlan's novel *Slow Burn*:

> Earlier that night a man's brains had been blown out.

Or of Phyllis Moore's short story "The Things They Married":

> First, she married herself.

Beginnings and endings allow room for dramatic license, and for breaks in style.

• Short sentences can deliver a "bang" that long sentences cannot. They also help emphasize a point that might get glossed over in a longer sentence, and help create contrast by breaking up a series of longer sentences. The short sentence in the following example achieves all three of these effects:

> Charlotte knew the time had come to tell her boss how she really felt, to let him know that she wouldn't take it a second longer. She slammed open her door and marched down the hall, past the unbelieving faces of the secretaries, and right into her boss' office. She looked into his eyes, summoned all of her courage and took a deep breath.
> She couldn't speak.

Or consider this example from Ralph Ellison's short story "Battle Royal":

> It goes a long way back, some twenty years. All my life I had been looking for something, and everywhere I turned someone tried to tell me what it was. I accepted their answers too, though they were often in contradiction and even self-contradictory. I was naïve.

The final sentence in this example would not have the same impact if it were as long as the sentences that preceded it.

• Short sentences can work well in the midst of dialogue exchanges, helping to move the action at a fast clip. Consider this example from Raymond Carver's short story "Night School":

> My marriage had just fallen apart. I couldn't find a job. I had another girl. But she wasn't in town. So I was at a bar having a glass of beer, and two women were sitting a few stools down, and one of them began to talk to me.
> "You have a car?"
> "I do, but it's not here," I said.
> My wife had the car. I was staying at my parents' place. I used their car sometimes. But tonight I was walking.

Carver was master of the short sentence, and his talents are on display here. Notice how he also uses short sentences preceding and following the dialogue exchange. At first glance these four-word sentences might seem juvenile; but they achieve the desired effect, each hammering home a significant point, and doing so in rapid succession.

• Short sentences can be used to keep the pace moving at a fast clip in general. This might be necessary, for example, in an action sequence:

> He turned the corner and sprinted down the alley. They were getting closer, fifty feet behind him. He kicked at the door. It wasn't giving. He put his shoulder to it. It gave with a groan and he stumbled inside. Stairs went up and down. He could hear them coming. He had to choose.

• On a more sophisticated level, short sentences can be used to complement the overall intention of the text. Consider this example from Flannery O'Connor's short story "The Lame Shall Enter First":

> Sheppard kept his intense blue eyes fixed on him. The boy's future was written in his face. He would be a banker. No, worse. He would operate a small loan company.

The short sentences capture the feeling of Sheppard's thought process. Each stop represents another twist in his thoughts, his reaching another conclusion. We actually feel him thinking as he goes, each period hammering it home. The time it allows us between thoughts is crucial, since Sheppard's conclusions change with every thought: we need time to digest. Without the periods, the observations would blur, and we wouldn't feel the thought process. Because of them, we feel he's thinking long and hard about the boy.

Camus also uses short sentences to great effect in the opening of his work *The Stranger*:

> Maman died today. Or yesterday maybe, I don't know. I got a telegram from the home: "Mother deceased. Funeral tomorrow.

Faithfully yours." That doesn't mean anything. Maybe it was yesterday.

The short sentences here serve many purposes. To begin with, these are the opening lines of the book and help to draw readers in quickly; they establish what will be the overall tone and style of the entire book; and on the more sophisticated level (which a master like Camus would have had in mind) they complement the overall meaning and intention of the text. The feeling evoked is clipped, matter-of-fact. Throughout *The Stranger* the narrator is also matter-of-fact about his mother's death, which turns out to be the crux of the story, and even the unnamed reason he is put to death. To further his intention, Camus immediately quotes a telegram, in which the short sentences mimic the short sentences of the narrator. (Keep in mind, though, that the above example is a translation from the French; quoting literature in translation—such as *The Stranger*—is inherently problematic, since numerous translators punctuate to their own fancy. That said, translators can only change a text so much, and Camus' intention remains.)

Hemingway was another master of the short sentence. Consider this example from his short story "Soldier's Home":

He did not want any consequences. He did not want any consequences ever again. He wanted to live along without any consequences. Because he did not really need a girl. The army had taught him that. It was all right to pose as though you had to have a girl. Nearly everybody did that. But it wasn't true. You did not need a girl. That was the funny thing.

With an author like Hemingway, the period is never used heavily for its own sake, but always because it serves a greater purpose. In this case, each period hammers home a thought in the soldier's head, and does so in such a way to suggest his being deeply affected by the war, even shell-shocked. The repetition of the content ("consequences" used three times in the first three sentences) also helps to achieve this effect.

Rick Moody is a gifted modern author known for his bold experimentation with prose and style. His book *Purple America*, for instance, begins with a sentence that stretches for *pages* before reaching a period. Consider the below example from his novel *The Ice Storm* that, ironically, displays his abundant use of the period:

> No answering machines. And no call waiting. No Caller I.D. No compact disc recorders or laser discs or holography or cable television or MTV. No multiplex cinemas or word processors or laser printers or modems. No virtual reality.

He could have chosen to separate these thoughts with merely a comma, or even a semicolon. By choosing to use periods, he allows each to sink in, more effectively cutting us off from the modern world.

THE DANGER OF OVERUSE

There is a major distinction between using periods heavily for a stylistic purpose (as explored above) and *over*using them, which results in poor writing. Newspaper and magazine writers tend to slip into this style, since this is how they've been trained to write. In book form, though, overusing periods is displeasing, as it creates a feeling of choppiness.

With each new sentence, a reader prepares to ride a wave, to entertain a new thought and have it carried through to its proper end. Readers don't want the wave to crash before they've had a proper ride. If jerked in and out of new thoughts, they will feel jostled, and be less likely to dig in for the long haul. Beginning a new sentence is a microcosm of beginning a new book: it takes effort. The effort is minute, but it's there. With several hundred pages before them, readers do not want to have to stop and start every few words. They want to settle in.

For example:

> He talked to the manager. She recommended a book. He looked it through. He liked it. He bought it.

Such a series of short sentences feels childlike—particularly if the content is banal, as it is here. Most writers will not resort to such extremes, yet there are times in a work when writers can get tired and slip. They might get caught up in the plot, characters, scene, and in the excitement not realize they overuse periods. Upon editing, it is important to keep an eye open for this, for a cluster of short sentences doing stylistic damage.

The real threat is not a sentence being short, but being short of content. A short sentence, if handled well, can convey more than an entire page—likewise, a long sentence can convey nothing. One must be watchful for short sentences that, in context, convey little, are incomplete thoughts, and that are unsatisfying. Sentences mustn't lean too heavily on one another, at least not without a purpose.

Perhaps more significant (and subtle) is learning to identify when a long sentence is too short—when a period comes too quickly in a longer sentence. Just because a sentence is long doesn't mean it's long enough. It can affect the reader only slightly, or even unconsciously. But the effect adds up. It is the crack in the windshield that starts to spread.

A short sentence can be satisfactory. But being satisfactory is not your goal as a writer; your goal is to be a master of the form. To do so means to agonize over every sentence and to ask yourself, among other things, if it needs to be longer. It could need to be longer in its own right, such as:

> She bought a dress.
> She used her last dollar to buy the dress for her mother.

Or it could need to be longer as a result of combining it with what follows (or what came before). Such as:

> She bought a dress. It was from her favorite store.
> She bought a dress from her favorite store.

Neither of these are necessarily "correct." Either example could work. It all depends on context, and on the effect you are trying to achieve. What's important is that, whatever route you decide to go, you do so as a result of deliberate choice.

> "In writing, punctuation plays the role of body language. It helps readers hear you the way you want to be heard."
>
> —RUSSELL BAKER

HOW TO UNDERUSE IT

Just as authors have used the period to great effect, so have authors deliberately underused it (creating longer sentences) to great effect.

Sometimes a certain effect can only be evoked by a long sentence—sometimes it is even necessary. A few possibilities:

- Long sentences—like short sentences—can work well at the beginning or ending of a chapter or book, for the same reasons outlined above: beginnings and endings allow poetic license, and a longer opening or ending can engage readers, allow them to settle in (or out). Like the opening and closing shots of a film (which are often much longer), readers are open for anything at those precious moments, and thus more willing to allow an unusual style. (We'll show an example of this later, from Faulkner's *Absalom, Absalom!*)

- A stream-of-consciousness effect (thoughts unraveling on the page in real time) can be achieved by using a longer sentence:

  I woke up this morning and knew what I had to do but then the phone rang and it was Shirley and she was on to her favorite topic and before I knew it I was hungry and burnt the toast again and had to go out for breakfast which left me no time at all to turn to the paper.

As you can see, stream of consciousness is chaotic; it unravels uncensored and thus has a "real time" feel. Few devices help create this effect more than the absence of the period. But this style is also suffocating. Unless there's an excellent reason, it should only be used in special cases.

- Long sentences (like short sentences) can be used to help capture a viewpoint. For example, they could portray an obsessive character, one whose mind wanders and who thinks in a way that can only be conveyed by long sentences:

I counted 29 dollars, but my manager told me it was 28 and that I was a dollar short, a dollar short, but I counted 29 and I counted three times and I don't trust him and I don't think I was a dollar short, even though he said it was, I know because I counted, I counted three times.

This is highly stylistic, and can't be maintained for long without driving readers crazy. But the long sentence here captures a breathless, neurotic feeling that short sentences could not.

• If you find yourself having difficulty differentiating viewpoints and narration styles of two characters in your work, one solution is to simply shorten the sentences of one character and lengthen those of the other. The difference will be immediately apparent. This is a quick fix, and won't always be appropriate, but the principle is important, as it demonstrates the power inherent in the placement of a period. In his brilliant novel *The River Warren*, modern author Kent Meyers portrays multiple character viewpoints, changing his style radically (and his use of the period) each time he does. Here's an example from his character Pop Bottle Pete's viewpoint:

Winter is cold. Not summer. Summer is when I find the bottles. And rocks. Rocks are like bottles.

Compare this to the viewpoint of another character, Jeff Gruber:

Twelve miles from Cloten on my way back from Duluth I stopped my car at a wayside rest on top of the bluffs above the river and looked down at the valley.

The drastic difference in sentence length helps establish the two different viewpoints.

• Intention. In the hands of a master, long sentences can reflect the very purpose and intention of the work. Consider this example from Faulkner's *Absalom, Absalom!* which is also the opening sentence of the novel:

> From a little after two o'clock until almost sundown of the long still hot weary dead September afternoon they sat in what Miss Coldfield still called the office because her father had called it that—a dim hot airless room with the blinds all closed and fastened for forty-three summers because when she was a girl someone had believed that light and moving air carried heat and that dark was always cooler, and which (as the sun shone fuller and fuller on that side of the house) became latticed with yellow slashes full of dust motes which Quentin thought of as being flecks of the dead old dried paint itself blown inward from the scaling blinds as wind might have blown them.

This single sentence lets us know we will be embarking on a read unlike any other, one that defies all rules. Faulkner doesn't let up, maintaining the style throughout the text. Considered one of the greatest novels of the twentieth century, this is truly a work synonymous with its placement of the period. In the hands of a lesser writer, it would be a disaster (and I wouldn't recommend it), yet Faulkner pulls it off. The style becomes one and the same with its characters, locale, time period: a heavy world, like the sentences, suffocating to enter and suffocating to survive.

Let's look at another Faulkner example, this one from his short story "That Evening Sun":

> Monday is no different from any other weekday in Jefferson now. The streets are paved now, and the telephone and electric companies are cutting down more and more of the shade trees—the water

oaks, the maples and locusts and elms—to make room for iron poles bearing clusters of bloated and ghostly and bloodless grapes, and we have a city laundry which makes the rounds on Monday morning, gathering the bundles of clothes into bright-colored, specially-made motor cars: the soiled wearing of a whole week now flees apparitionlike behind alert and irritable electric horns, with a long diminishing noise of rubber and asphalt like tearing silk, and even the Negro women who still take in white people's washing after the old custom, fetch and deliver it in automobiles.

In the second, incredibly long, sentence, Faulkner encapsulates all of Monday, makes us experience the routine of the entire day. He also uses the excuse of describing a Monday to actually describe an entire town, the changes it's undergoing, the habits of its people, and even the race relations. Note also the tremendous contrast in length between the first and second sentence, which proves that Faulkner has deliberately chosen to lengthen this particular sentence.

The main point is that there must be a reason for such usage. It cannot be done haphazardly, or merely for the sake of being stylistic. If you do employ it, your chances of success are greater if you limit it to a short stretch—for example, for a minor character. Most writers grasp this, and will not craft overly long sentences. What the everyday writer can take away from this is to become aware of the subtle effect of a sentence that goes slightly too long, and the cumulative effect this will have on the work. Most of the time the question the writer needs to ask himself is: Is this sentence one thought too long? Can this one sentence be broken down into two? (Just as you must ask if two shorter sentences can be combined.) Are there multiple ideas—particularly powerful ideas—in one sentence? Is there a risk of something getting lost in its length? Is it worth the risk? Is the period too powerful of a divider? Should you instead resort to lesser dividers, such as the colon or semicolon? (We will explore these in later chapters.)

THE DANGER OF UNDERUSE

If reading a series of too-short sentences is like traveling in choppy waters, then reading a series of too-long sentences is like riding a wave that rolls and rolls but never, satisfyingly, crashes. Most readers feel as if they're gasping for breath when reading long sentences; they have a harder time following the idea and are more likely to put a book down sooner.

Nobody wants to read a sentence like this, one that never ends, that goes on and on without giving the reader a rest between thoughts or ideas or a chance to catch his breath and go onto the next sentence which could seem like a distant goal by the time this sentence is through.

There are many reasons a writer might fall into the trap of crafting too-long sentences:

• On the simplest level, the writer may not know how to end a sentence, may not have properly grasped that a sentence serves primarily to put forth a single idea. Too-long sentences are often the result of a writer trying to cram too many ideas into a single sentence.

• A writer might craft too-long sentences out of a fear of letting a sentence conclude, an insecurity that the sentence is not complete enough in its own right, that the idea put forth is not satisfying enough. This writer wants to cover his bases with multiple ideas, so that no one can accuse him of being insubstantial.

• Academics and scholars tend to use long sentences, as they are used to reading longer sentences themselves. They are able to retain many concepts in one sitting, to hang on to a concept while it twists and turns through many other concepts; their mistake is assuming that a lay reader can do the same (or even wants to). This is rarely the case.

• Sometimes too-long sentences are employed simply for effect, by young writers experimenting with the form, for example, trying to mimic Faulkner. In such a case, they mistake style for being stylistic, and call attention to the writing instead of the content.

• Too-long sentences might be created out of a desire to sound more sophisticated. Some writers fear crafting shorter sentences will make their text read childlike, so they overcompensate, increasing sentence length until they end up doing stylistic damage in the reverse direction.

Regardless of your motive, you must realize that nothing is gained by lengthening a sentence just for the sake of it—on the contrary, you lose. Less is more. Years ago, readers had a greater attention span and a greater capacity to easily ride the twists and turns of a long sentence. Today, less so. The modern-day reader does not want to exercise his brain through a paragraph-long sentence, and the ideas put forth in such a sentence will likely be lost. Writing is about simplicity and clarity, and the best way to achieve this is to allow each thought its own sentence.

> "There's not much to be said about the period except that most writers don't reach it soon enough."
>
> —WILLIAM ZINSSER

CONTEXT

One of the biggest mistakes a writer can make is evaluating a sentence in its own right, instead of in context with the sentences around it. In the midst of a series of long sentences, a short sentence can be needed, whether for impact, for variety, or to make a thought stand out. Likewise, in the midst of a paragraph of short sentences, a long sentence can be needed, whether to add variety, fluidity, or to trim the edges off a childlike feel. Conversely, sometimes a shorter (or longer) sentence is needed precisely because it is surrounded by shorter (or longer) sentences, in order to maintain consistency. You set the bar when you dictate the style, and you must be prepared to offer at least a modicum of uniformity—or to break it with good intention. A long sentence subconsciously suggests a long one will follow; if a short sentence follows, it will be in the spotlight. Sometimes this is preferable, if you want to emphasize a point. But it must be deliberate. Ultimately, you must remember that a sentence is only short or long in context. In the world of Camus' *The Stranger*, an eight-word sentence can be long; in the world of Faulkner's *Absalom, Absalom!* a one-hundred-word sentence can be short.

Alternately, writers can get blinded by context. One can get caught up in the context of a paragraph or scene and not stop to consider if that sentence stands well on its own. Sentences help each other hide: one can get away with a short sentence amid a cluster of short sentences. Don't allow yourself to get blinded by your own momentum; just as you must evaluate each sentence in context, so must you put a magnifying glass to each sentence in its own right.

This is a conundrum for the writer. On the one hand, you must establish a certain style and maintain it, which means that if writing long sentences you must continue to write long sentences, and if writing short sentences you must continue to write short sentences;

on the other hand, long sentence after long sentence (or short sentence after short sentence) quickly becomes staid, lifeless. Stylistic variety is not only wanted, but needed, for all of the reasons outlined above. Such variety, though, doesn't give you an excuse to avoid establishing an overall style, such as Camus did for *The Stranger* or Faulkner did for *Absalom, Absalom!* You must find a way to establish your style, but then break it when need be, offering constant variety to keep the prose lively and unexpected. It is a delicate balance, and one you must perpetually struggle with.

Consider the following example from James Joyce's short story "Araby":

> When the short days of winter came, dusk fell before we had well eatern our dinners. When we met in the street the houses had grown sombre. The space of sky above us was the colour of ever-changing violet and towards it the lamps of the street lifted their feeble lanterns. The cold air stung us and we played till our bodies glowed. Our shouts echoed in the silent street. The career of our play brought us through the dark muddy lanes behind the houses, where we ran the gauntlet of the rough tribes from the cottages, to the back doors of the dark dripping gardens where odours arose from the ashpits, to the dark odorous stables where a coachman smoothed and combed the horse or shook music from the buckled harness. When we returned to the street, light from the kitchen windows had filled the areas.

Look at what Joyce does here for stylstic variety. His first five sentences are short, and his sixth sentence is, in comparison, incredibly long, nearly five times longer than the sentences that preceded it. In the hands of a master like Joyce, this is not accidental. The sixth sentence talks about the time they spent playing, and its length conveys the feeling of their getting lost in play, of their play stretching forever. Indeed, the final sentence confirms this, informing us that it is dark by the time they finished. By varying his sentence length here, he is able to subtly compare and contrast these images, to build up to an important image, and then come back down from it. For Joyce, stylistic context is paramount.

You must also consider the placement of a punctuation mark in context with other punctuation marks around it. Period placement takes on a whole new meaning when commas, semicolons, colons, and dashes (to be discussed in later chapters) are nearby. These friends of the period can rescue it, can serve as rest stops along the way. By allowing the reader a chance to rest, a semicolon, for example, can take the pressure off a period, make it no longer feel like a distant objective on the horizon. Consider Elizabeth Barrett Browning's *Sonnets from the Portuguese*, "Sonnet 22":

> When our two souls stand up erect and strong,
> Face to face, silent, drawing nigh and nigher,
> Until the lengthening wings break into fire
> At either curvèd point—what bitter wrong
> Can the earth do to us, that we should not long
> Be here contented? Think.

The contrast of that final sentence is amazing, especially following on the heels of such a long and stylistically varied sentence. The period hammers home the thought, forces the reader to stop and truly think.

In the hands of a master like Shakespeare, the context of period placement and sentence length takes on layers of meanings—indeed, is taken to a whole new level. Let's look, for instance, at *Macbeth*. In a portion of Macbeth's soliloquy at the end of act 1, he debates with himself over whether he should murder his king:

> He's here in double trust:
> First, as I am his kinsman and his subject,
> Strong both against the deed; then, as his host,
> Who should against his murtherer shut the door,
> Not bear the knife myself. Besides, this Duncan
> Hath borne his faculties so meek, hath been
> So clear in his great office, that his virtues
> Will plead like angels, trumpet-tongu'd, against
> The deep damnation of his taking-off;
> And pity, like a naked new-born babe,
> Striding the blast, or heaven's cherubin, hors'd
> Upon the sightless couriers of the air,
> Shall blow the horrid deed in every eye,
> That tears shall drown the wind.

As Macbeth takes a journey, so does his speech and its punctuation. Note the increasingly long sentences as Macbeth delves deeper into the horror and chaos of the contemplated deed. The first complete sentence is nearly five lines. The next sentence is over nine lines. And if, for the purpose of analyzing this speech, we consider the semicolons and colons to serve the same purpose as periods (which they could, depending on the actor), then we see even more clearly the escalation of sentence length. While Macbeth begins with a simple five-word phrase ("He's here in double trust"), he culminates with a thirty-six-word sentence (ending with ". . . drown the wind"). The sentence length mimics the chaotic mind of a would-be murderer. As a result of the period placement alone, you can feel Macbeth's momentum build, with the longest sentence bringing us to the very heart of murder. Indeed, that long sentence is the turning point. When it's over, Macbeth comes to the conclusion that he has "no spur / To prick the sides of my intent. . . ." He's realized it would be wrong to kill his king. And that final sentence wouldn't be "long" if a shorter sentence hadn't preceded it.

One must also consider the line breaks here. The line break in poetry is the invisible pause, and might be considered stronger than a comma, yet not quite as strong as a semicolon. Sometimes poets play against this pause, breaking a line where seemingly there should be no break—but even in such case it is deliberate. The line break is an amazingly subtle device, suggesting a pause instead of demanding one. In the hands of the right poet, the line break can help to emphasize a word or idea at the end of one line before rushing to the next; it can offer a moment of reflection. Sometimes that moment will be great, while at others it will suggest only the slightest of pauses. Shakespeare, of course, wrote mostly in iambic pentameter, so for him the line breaks took on extra significance; some Shakespeare scholars insist that line breaks are also clues for actors, demanding they take a beat.

For Shakespeare, sentence length was not about a single thought: it was about the context of the paragraph (or stanza), the context of the moment in the play, the context of the scene, and the context of the thought process of the character. Shakespeare was good enough to hold an entire play in his head at once, and to consider the effect the placement of a period could have on a period he'd placed two thousand lines before. He was truly a master of context.

(Keep in mind, though, that analyzing Shakespeare's punctuation is also problematic: it is, at best, a guess. While this example comes from the authoritative Riverside edition, there is no definitive source that proves precisely what Shakespeare's original punctuation was.)

WHAT YOUR USE OF THE PERIOD
REVEALS ABOUT YOU

Often it's hard for a writer to take a step back and gain true objectivity on his own work. Punctuation, though, never lies. Whether you like it or not, punctuation reveals the writer. Analyzing your punctuation forces you to take a step back, to gain a bird's-eye view of your own writing. It reveals a tremendous amount about your style, and about your approach to writing.

Let's take a step back now and gain that bird's-eye view. We will listen to the punctuation—not the content—and let it tell us its story. It always has a good story to tell.

The writer who overuses the period (creating consistently short sentences) tends to be action oriented. He is fast paced and keeps readers in mind, as he strives to grab their attention and keep the work moving. This is to his benefit. Unfortunately, he is also likely to have not yet developed a good ear for language, for the subtleties of sentence length, style, rhythm, and pitch. This writer is impatient; he is too desperate to grab the reader, and resorts to a quick-paced style to do so, rather than crafting content that is inherently dramatic. He needs confidence, and indeed is probably young in his career. He will more likely be a commercial writer, more interested in plot than characterization, and might hail from a journalistic background, or at least be an avid reader of newspapers and magazines.

The writer who underuses the period (creating consistently long sentences) falls into two categories: either he is an amateur who thinks in an uncensored, chaotic manner, or he is a seasoned writer who crafts too-long sentences deliberately. If the latter, he is likely to be literary, to take chances and aspire to create rich prose. This bodes well. Unfortunately, though, he is also too focused on word craft, likely at the expense of pacing and plot. Indeed, he writes more for himself than for readers, which can lead to self-indulgence. He is likely to be too stylized, even lean toward pretentiousness. He is also likely to use advanced words for their own sake, and to rely too heavily on colons and semicolons (more on this later).

EXERCISES

Throughout the book I will give you exercises that enable you to experiment with sentence construction. What you are really experimenting with is different approaches to writing, which in turn will spark different ways of thinking and even creative ideas. The ramifications should lead far beyond the sentence itself.

Let's grapple with the period, and see how it can influence your writing.

• Start a new novel (or short story), and let the opening sentence run at least one page long. Where does this lead you? How did you compensate? Did you find a new narration style? Did not stopping allow you more creative freedom? Can you apply this technique elsewhere in your writing?

• Start a new novel (or short story), and don't let any sentence run more than six words. Where does this lead you? How did you compensate? Did you find a new narration style? Did the constant stopping allow you more creative freedom? Can you apply this technique elsewhere in your writing?

• Imagine a character who thinks in long sentences. Who would this be? Why would he think this way? Capture his viewpoint on the page, using long sentences. Do the long sentences help bring out who he is? Do they make the text feel one and the same with the character? Can you apply this technique elsewhere in your writing?

• Imagine a character who thinks in short sentences. Who would this be? Why would he think this way? Capture his viewpoint on the page, using short sentences. Do the short sentences help bring out who he is? Do they make the text feel one and the same with the character? Can you apply this technique elsewhere in your writing?

• Choose a short sentence from your work, ideally one already in a cluster of short sentences. Find a way to make it longer without combining it with the material preceding or following it—in other words, add to the idea in the sentence. See how far you can stretch it. Could there be any more to this idea before you go on to the next sentence? Are you harvesting individual sentences for all they're worth? Can you apply this technique elsewhere in your work?

• Choose a series of short sentences from your work, possibly in an area where you feel the action moves too quickly. Combine two sentences, adding material to each if need be. Then combine three. How does it change the flow of the paragraph? Of the scene? What do you gain? Can you apply this technique elsewhere in your work?

• Choose a long sentence from your manuscript, ideally one already in a cluster of long sentences. To decide if it needs shortening, consider the following: Does it comprise several ideas? Is it hard to grasp? Is it hard to catch one's breath? Does its length match other sentence lengths? Find a way to shorten it, without combining it with the material in the sentence preceding or following it. How much can you shorten it? Was there any extraneous material here? Can you apply this technique elsewhere in your work?

• Choose a series of long sentences from your manuscript, ideally in a place where the pace slows. Choose two sentences with similar ideas and find a way to combine them, shortening each in the process. Now try it with three sentences. What did you have to sacrifice in order to combine them? How does it change the flow of the paragraph? Of the scene? What do you gain? Can you apply this technique elsewhere in your work?

• Choose a paragraph where all of the sentences are of drastically varying length. Adjust the sentences (by either shortening or lengthening) to make them all of uniform length. How does it read now? What do you gain by this? What do you lose? Can you apply this technique elsewhere in your work?

• Choose a paragraph where all of the sentences are of uniform length. Adjust the sentences (by either shortening or lengthening) to make the sentence lengths radically contrast with one another. How does it read now? What do you gain by this? What do you lose? Can you apply this technique elsewhere in your work?

• Take all the principles you've just learned, and apply them to any page in your manuscript. First read it aloud, focusing on how the sentences read individually and on whether any feel too long or short. Use the principles you've learned to identify sentences that will need shortening or lengthening. If you can fix them by simply using a period, great. If you'll also need to employ a comma, semicolon, colon, or other marks, then read on.

THE
COMMA

(*the Speed Bump*)

> If you can master the uses of the comma—or even the basic
> ones—no other mark can hold any terrors for you.
>
> —HARRY SHAW,
> *Punctuate It Right!*

THE COMMA IS the speed bump of the punctuation world. With
its power to pause, the comma controls the ebb and flow of a sentence, its rhythm, its speed. Based on frequency alone, the comma
wields tremendous influence, outnumbering the period by at least
three to one, and outnumbering other punctuation marks by at
least five to one. And yet, paradoxically, it is also the mark most
open to interpretation. The comma has few hard rules, and as a
result is the mark most often misused.

The comma can be used to divide. "The word comma is derived
from Greek *komma* (clause), which came from *koptein* (to cut off).
Indeed, a comma normally does 'cut off' one part of a sentence from
another," says Harry Shaw says in *Punctuate It Right!* In this sense,
the comma can control meaning itself, since the same sentence cut
in different ways takes on entirely new meaning.

Yet the comma can also connect. Two sentences can become one
by virtue of a comma, and a sentence can be made longer in its own

right by tacking on a comma. In this capacity, the comma is a people person, a middleman. It likes to be connected, and to make connections. Both divider and connector, the comma is schizophrenic.

The comma is supremely important if for no other reason than its relationship to the period. Without the comma, the period is often left in the cold, waiting at the end of a long sentence without a rest stop. To grasp the comma's influence, imagine a long sentence without any commas:

> A sentence like this without any commas makes it nearly impossible for the reader to know when to pause if not when to stop and also makes him feel as if the period cannot come soon enough indeed should have come several moments ago.

You have to reread it several times just to figure out its natural rhythm and grasp its meaning. Why would you, as a writer, want to make the reader work twice as hard? With the proper use of the comma, you won't have to.

HOW TO USE IT

The comma is probably the hardest of all punctuation marks to master. Not only is it the most flexible, not only are its uses the most varied, but it also carries few rules and has been used (and not used) by great authors in many different ways.

That said, you can learn to master the comma. Its creative uses are many, and they must each be examined carefully:

• To connect. The comma can connect several half ideas (or clauses) into one grand idea (the sentence). It is the glue that holds a sentence together. If a short sentence is lacking in fullness of meaning, a comma can step in to connect it to the sentences that follow:

I sat on a bench. I opened my book. I removed the bookmark.

I sat on a bench, opened my book, and removed the bookmark.

The commas here have connected three infantile sentences into one more elegant sentence.

- To provide clarity. If a sentence conveys several ideas, a comma can help distinguish them. Without a comma, you risk readers reading from one clause to the other without grasping where one idea ends and another begins. Subsequently, each idea won't have the impact it could otherwise, won't have the proper time and space to be digested. Consider:

She told me I looked like an old boyfriend of hers then turned and walked away.

Here we feel no pause between the first clause and the second, no time to digest. One comma, though, can make all the difference:

She told me I looked like an old boyfriend of hers, then turned and walked away.

Now we feel the proper pause, can fully process each of these clauses. In this capacity, commas act like buoys in the sea, letting us know when we're leaving one zone and entering another.

- To pause. This is what the comma was built for, where it really shines. A comma allows the reader to catch his breath (as he would if reading aloud), and prevents a long sentence from reading like stream of consciousness. For example, read the following sentence aloud:

> He raised his rifle cocked it adjusted his neck and had the deer in his sights but when he went to pull the trigger his hand started shaking again just like it had every day for the last two weeks or maybe three he couldn't be sure.

With no chance to pause, the reader hopelessly builds momentum until he crashes into the period. It is the equivalent of taking one huge breath and seeing how much you can say before you burst. Sentences were not meant to be read that way, and should not be written that way. A few commas, though, can transform the reading experience:

> He raised his rifle, cocked it, adjusted his neck, and had the deer in his sights, but when he went to pull the trigger his hand started shaking again, just like it had every day for the last two weeks, or maybe three, he couldn't be sure.

• The comma can be used to indicate a passing of time, particularly in creative writing. This is something I rarely see employed well. Consider:

> John thought about that and said . . .

Although technically correct, we don't feel a pause here between John's thinking and his speaking. But if we add a comma:

> John thought about that, and said . . .

Now we feel the moment. It is subtle, but a well-placed comma adds just enough time in a scene to make a difference, one that works unconsciously on the reader.

Consider this example from Jean Toomer's short story "Blood-Burning Moon":

Up from the skeleton walls, up from the rotting floor boards and the solid hand-hewn beams of oak of the pre-war cotton factory, dusk came.

The commas here, particularly since they encapsulate such long clauses, make us really pause, make us feel the approach of dusk.

Lynne Truss addresses this point with an apt story in *Eats, Shoots & Leaves:* "Thurber was once asked by a correspondent: 'Why did you have a comma in the sentence, "After dinner, the men went into the living room"?' And his answer was probably one of the loveliest things ever said about punctuation. 'This particular comma,' Thurber explained, 'was Ross's way of giving the men time to push back their chairs and stand up.'"

• The comma can alter the very meaning of a sentence. Consider:

The windows with the glass treatment are holding up well.

The windows, with the glass treatment, are holding up well.

In the latter sentence it's understood that the windows are holding up well *because* of the glass treatment; in the former, it can be understood that the windows, which were created with a glass treatment, are holding up well in general. The entire meaning of the sentence changes, simply due to the comma placement.

• The comma can be used to offset a clause or idea, to allow it to stand out when it might otherwise be lost. Consider:

Taking medicine and eating well coupled with exercise can help assure a healthy life.

Taking medicine and eating well, coupled with exercise, can help assure a healthy life.

In the latter example, the commas force us to pause before and after "coupled with exercise," offsetting it and emphasizing a point that might have been glossed over otherwise.

• The comma can be used to maximize word economy. Placing a comma in the right spot can enable you to delete several words. For example:

I liked chocolate and she liked vanilla.

I liked chocolate, she vanilla.

All in all, the comma has so many different creative uses and can enhance a work creatively in so many ways, that it can be detrimental *not* to use it. Like its cousin the period, it is one of the few marks of punctuation that must be used throughout.

Let's look at the comma in the hands of a master. Joseph Conrad, in *Heart of Darkness*, uses commas to create a memorable setting:

A narrow and deserted street in deep shadow, high houses, innumerable windows with venetian blinds, a dead silence, grass sprouting between the stones, imposing carriage archways right and left, immense double doors standing ponderously ajar.

It's amazing what he achieves in one sentence, all with the use of commas. He has created an entire setting. Each comma not only helps increase the list, but also separates, gives us time to ponder each aspect of the setting. By inserting all of this information under the umbrella of a single sentence, divided only by commas, Conrad asks us to experience this entire setting as one thought, asks us to realize the whole picture of this desolate place in one unremitting image.

Here's another example, this from the opening sentence of J. M. Coetzee's novel *Disgrace:*

For a man of his age, fifty-two, divorced, he has, to his mind, solved the problem of sex rather well.

This example comes at the suggestion of critically acclaimed novelist and writing teacher Paul Cody, and is an example that he teaches repeatedly. He offers this analysis: "This is a seemingly simple sentence, broken into six parts, using only commas. The language is spare, but the use of the commas give the sentence great power and irony. The reader has to pause five times, and the sense of the man is that he's a control freak, he's got everything in order, he's figured it all out. But each part of the sentence undermines what he's saying. We know he's got it all wrong, that he's figured out nothing, that he has no understanding whatsoever of sex, love, the human heart. And each comma makes us pause, is a nail in the coffin of his soul, his isolation."

James Baldwin uses the comma heavily in his story "Sonny's Blues":

I read about it in the paper, in the subway, on my way to work. I read it, and I couldn't believe it, and I read it again. Then perhaps I just stared at it, at the newsprint spelling out his name, spelling out the story. I stared at it in the swinging lights of the subway car, and in the faces and bodies of the people, and in my own face, trapped in the darkness which roared outside.

The abundant commas here reflect the narrator's experience as he's reading the piece, reflect his being shocked by the news, and needing multiple pauses to take it all in. John Cheever uses the comma for a different effect in his story "The Enormous Radio":

Jim and Irene Westcott were the kind of people who seem to strike that satisfactory average of income, endeavor, and respectability that is reached by the statistical reports in college alumni bulletins. They were the parents of two young children, they had been married nine years, they lived on the twelfth floor of an apartment house near Sutton Place, they went to the theatre on an average of 10.3 times a year, and they hoped someday to live in Westchester.

The commas here mimic the feeling of detailing items in a list. Except the grocery list here is their lives, which have been planned out too perfectly, too methodically. The commas subtly hint at this.

In her story "What I Know," Victoria Lancelotta uses commas to complement the content:

This is the sort of air that sticks, the kind you want to pull off you, away from your skin, or wipe away in great sluicing motions and back into the water where it surely belongs, because this is not the sort of air that anyone could breathe. You could die, drown, trying to breathe this.

We almost feel as if we're suffocating, drowning in her commas, which is exactly the type of air she's trying to describe.

In one of the great poems of the twentieth century, "The Waste Land," T. S. Eliot opens with a comma-laden sentence:

> April is the cruelest month, breeding
> Lilacs out of the dead land, mixing
> Memory and desire, stirring
> Dull roots with spring rain.

Eliot could have chosen to separate each of these images into several sentences, but instead he chose to keep them together, in one long sentence, connected by commas. By doing so, he forces us to take in the image of April in one long thought, and to fully realize how cruel it is.

Perhaps because of this reason, because of its ability to connect several images in one thought, you'll find that the comma is often used in literature when introducing a character. Consider this example from Saul Bellow's "Leaving the Yellow House":

> You couldn't help being fond of Hattie. She was big and cheerful, puffy, comic, boastful, with a big round back and stiff, rather long legs.

From Ella Leffland's "The Linden Tree":

> Giulio was a great putterer. You could always see him sweeping the front steps or polishing the doorknobs, stopping to gossip with the neighbors. He was a slight, pruny man of sixty-eight, perfectly bald, dressed in heavy trousers, a bright sports shirt with a necktie, and an old man's sweater-jacket, liver-colored and hanging straight to the knees.

The commas here enable you take in all of the character traits at once, to absorb this person in one image, as you might do if meeting him in person. Notice also the varying of style here: both of these examples begin with short, comma-less sentences, and culminate in long, comma-laden sentences. Not only does this help to create contrast, to break up the rhythm and style, but it further demonstrates that the author's use of commas is deliberate.

> "It is a safe statement that a gathering of commas (except on certain lawful occasions, as in a list) is a suspicious circumstance."
> —H. W. AND F. G. FOWLER, *The King's English*

DANGER OF OVERUSE

The necessity of the comma causes writers to misuse it more than any other punctuation mark. The period is luckier in this respect, since it is appears less frequently and is less open to interpretation; the colon, semicolon, and dash are also lucky, as they can easily absent themselves from most works, and thus hide from heavy misuse. Yet the comma demands to be used—and used frequently—and this, together with the fact that it carries nebulous rules, makes it a prime target. And the main way writers misuse the comma is to *over*use it.

If there is anything worse than a work bereft of commas, it is one drowning in them. "Any one who finds himself putting down several commas close to one another should reflect that he is making himself disagreeable, and question his conscience, as severely as we ought to do about disagreeable conduct in real life," said the Fowler brothers in *The King's English* in 1905. This might be a bit extreme, but their point is well taken.

Overusing commas can create many problems:

• When a sentence is laden with commas, it slows to a crawl, makes readers feel as if they're plowing through quicksand. For example:

> The florist, the one with the red hair, who had the only shop in town, right on my corner, was having a sale, at least a partial sale, of her trees, which were half dead, and overpriced to begin with.

Readers don't want to have to stop several times to finish a single sentence. As a writer your foremost concern is keeping readers turning pages, and thus you must be keenly aware of when you're slowing the pace, and only do so for an excellent reason. This especially holds true if you're in a section of your work, like an action scene, where a fast pace is required.

• A comma pauses, qualifies, or divides a thought, but if done too frequently, the original thought can become lost. For example:

> We can eat our ice cream, soft, vanilla ice cream, with extra sprinkles, with those cherries on top, with whipped cream and hot fudge, in the living room.

The main point here was supposed to be that they could eat their ice cream in the living room. But with such a long aside, that point is all but lost. The commas, overused, distract to a fault.

> Some would say, in a manner of speaking, that, given the context of the Greek empire, and the context of world affairs, Alexander, in light of his time, was a great warrior.

The comma can be overused when qualifying, as in the above

example. When everything is qualified it creates a hesitant, uncon-fident feel to a work, as if the writer's afraid to say what he has to. Academics particularly fall prey to this. If we take out the qualifi-cations (and the commas they demand), the point is more bold, succinct:

Alexander was a great warrior.

Now a stance is taken and whether it's right or wrong, readers will admire it. Readers want strong arguments and strong opinions; they don't like writers who play it safe. There is a benefit to enter-taining one thought—particularly a complicated one—without interruption.

• Sometimes commas are simply unnecessary. Some sentences work with a comma, but also work equally well without one. If so, it is always preferable to omit it. For example:

He told me that, if I worked hard, he would give me Saturday off.

He told me that if I worked hard he would give me Saturday off.

Neither of these is "correct." It depends on your intent: if you really feel the need to emphasize the qualification of his working hard, then you need the commas. But if not, they can be removed. In writing, less is more, and you never want to slow the reader unless you have to.

HOW TO UNDERUSE IT

The comma is one of the only punctuation marks so widely used that its *omission* is a stylistic statement. Writers like Gertrude Stein and Cormac McCarthy are known for eschewing the comma, and books exist that never employed a single comma, notably Peter Carey's *True History of the Kelly Gang*, which won the 2001 Booker Prize. Why would a writer opt to ignore the friendly comma? What would he gain from it?

The reasons to underuse the comma are largely similar to the reasons not to overuse it. Yet there is a subtle difference between aiming not to *overuse* something and deliberately aiming to *underuse* it. In the former, you aim to avoid, or edit out, a problem; in the latter, you aim to deliberately craft something in a certain way. The benefits achieved will largely parallel each other, yet there are different reasons for doing so, and different approaches:

• You might abstain from commas in order to speed up the pace, particularly in a section where the work lags. Comma-less writing is as fast as it gets. It accelerates the rhythm, and in some instances this is necessary.

• There might be times when you want a sentence to be read as a single uninterrupted thought. In such a case, removing the comma creates the desired effect:

I checked the filter, and changed the water, and hit the button three times, and the damned thing still wasn't working.

I checked the filter and changed the water and hit the button three times and the damned thing still wasn't working.

Both of these are acceptable, but they offer different effects. The latter reads as if spoken all in one breath, and the writer might want this effect to indicate the narrator's exasperation, his letting it all out at once. It is a stylistic decision.

•The same holds true in dialogue, where the comma's impact is even more potent. You can, for example, omit commas in dialogue to indicate someone speaking all in one breath, or in a hurried manner. Consider:

"Make a right on 57th and a left on 3rd and a right on 80th and step on it because I'm ten minutes late."

This can also be used to indicate someone in the midst of a heated dialogue, who, for example, won't let the other person get a word in. Or it can be used to indicate a distracted person, or one who has no attention span and who rambles on uncensored.

• Omitting commas can help achieve a stream-of-consciousness feeling.

When one reads a long free-flowing sentence like this without any commas it gives the feeling of letting it all out uncensored which is exactly what the stream of consciousness writer is trying to achieve when crafting his work which he might consider a sort of calculated spontaneity.

Pausing is synonymous with thinking and calculation, and thus it is not surprising that the hallmark of stream-of-consciousness writing is a dearth of commas.

• You can omit commas in order to deliberately gloss over something important. Some writers like to make readers work, to not lay out everything; for them, the joy comes in forcing the reader to decipher their text. One way of doing this is to mention an important item merely as an afterthought, perhaps even sandwich it between unimportant items. Some writers aim to create sentences that, if you read late at night, you are likely to miss. They might drop bombshells this way and keep going; the story has changed and the reader does not know why, and needs to go back and reread. It is the understated approach, the antirevelation. And it can be facilitated by burying key information amid a comma-bereft sentence.

Let's look at some examples from literature. In her story "Kew Gardens," Virginia Woolf deliberately omits commas when describing the "flower-bed":

> From the oval-shaped flower-bed there rose perhaps a hundred stalks spreading into the heart-shaped or tongue-shaped leaves half-way up and unfurling at the tip red or blue or yellow petals marked with spots of colour raised upon the surface. . . .

This is stylized, and will be hard for most readers to digest; but Woolf must have felt that it furthered her intention, or else she would not have chosen to omit the commas. You might say that omitting the commas here allows the reader to take in the entire beauty of the flower bed in one breathless sweep.

In one of her most famous poems, "Sonnet 43," Elizabeth Barrett Browning avoids commas to great effect:

> How do I love thee? Let me count the ways.
> I love thee to the depth and breadth and height
> My soul can reach, when feeling out of sight
> For the ends of Being and ideal Grace.

Normally "depth and breadth and height" would be separated by commas; by ommitting them, Browning forces us to consider all three breathlessly, as if to further emphasize that there is no limit, or pause, to her love. Note also the varying of style here: she begins with two short sentences, the first culminating in a question mark, the second in a period, then follows with a long sentence. The variety gives us a fullness we would not have otherwise (more on this later, in the epilogue).

DANGER OF UNDERUSE

With all reward comes potential risks. If you go too far in your underuse of the comma, you run into other dangers and come full circle, back to the same problems that required you to implement the comma in the first place. A few potential pitfalls:

• On the most basic level, a sentence bereft of commas can be hard to understand. The main function of the comma is to clarify, and when commas are missing, readers can confuse one clause of a sentence with another. They will be forced to reread, to exert additional effort to figure out where the pauses should have been. For example:

> With three bolts two screwdrivers one hammer and a box of nails we went to the shop my uncle Harry's that is to see what we could do with the old red Buick.

With writing like this, readers can feel as if they're being sucked into a grammatical black hole, and put the work down. It's just not worth the extra effort.

• Every sentence has a certain rhythm to it, a certain "flow." Read a sentence aloud and you'll naturally hear where you must pause. Commas are the written version of that pause; they slow the language, and suggest a pause when need be. Removing them can send readers into a tailspin; they will plunge ahead, realizing something's amiss but unable to stop until they've crashed headlong into the period. The rhythm of the sentence will be ruined, and on some level readers will feel it. For example:

> She left the window open even though I told her not to and the cold air sent the old thermometer which was on the fritz to begin with into its final decline sending the heat to 96 degrees and increasing my oil bill which was already extravagant to over $1,000 for the month.

• Pauses can be necessary in the midst of dialogue. Without commas in dialogue, it reads as if a character speaks breathlessly, which can make the dialogue be interpreted differently than you had intended. You must carefully consider the weight of time in dialogue. For example:

> "If you want me to come, if you really do, I'll be happy to."

> "If you want me to come if you really do I'll be happy to."

Since this is contained within dialogue, neither of these are "wrong." It depends on how you'd like to convey your character's speech patterns. The former would be the most natural choice; the latter would be highly stylized, would indicate a more unusual speech, suggesting it is all uttered with one breath. This is fine—if deliberate. The problem comes when this is *not* deliberate, when a writer omits commas merely because he does not have a good ear for pauses within dialogue.

• If you'd like to convey more than one significant idea in a sentence and don't use commas for separation, you run the risk—even if grammatically correct—of the ideas blurring, and of the reader missing one or more of them. Consider:

The music had a profound effect on me and the seats gave me an entirely new perspective of the theater.

The music had a profound effect on me, and the seats gave me an entirely new perspective of the theater.

Again, both of these examples are acceptable, and both are grammatically correct. It goes back to the issue of intention. In the former example, without the comma, you run the risk of the reader glossing over the fact that the music had a profound effect on the narrator. In the latter example, the comma forces you to pause, to take that extra beat to consider the fact that the music had a profound effect on him.

- Without commas, an aside or qualification can become glossed over:

    She said she'd come over if it snows to help me build a fire in the fireplace.

    She said she'd come over, if it snows, to help me build a fire in the fireplace.

In the latter example, it is clear that she will only come over if it snows; in the former, the aside "if it snows" is not offset by commas and thus a reader won't pause before and after it. There is a greater chance that a reader—particularly a tired one—could gloss over it. You must decide whether that chance is worth it.

- A sentence can be perfectly acceptable without commas, yet the overall intention might be ambiguous. Inserting commas can alter meaning. Consider:

In sixteen days' time, the rebels will be here and we'll be ready to fight.

In sixteen days' time the rebels will be here, and we'll be ready to fight.

The effect is subtle. In the former example, the intention of the sentence is to describe what will happen in sixteen days; in the latter example, the intention is not time but the fact that the rebels will come at all. Something as seemingly minor as the placement of a comma can make all the difference.

> "The use of commas cannot be learned by rule. Not only does conventional practice vary from period to period, but good writers of the same period differ among themselves. . . . The correct use of the comma— if there is such a thing as 'correct' use—can only be acquired by common sense, observation and taste."
>
> —SIR ERNEST GOWERS

CONTEXT

No punctuation mark acts alone; every time you decide to employ one—especially the comma, which often allows you the choice of including or omitting it—you must take into account the effect it will have on the marks preceding and following it. For instance, when you use a comma, you lessen the effect of the period and semicolon. The comma steals the limelight. It slows the reader dramatically, and thus the stop sign no longer has such great impact.

In a sentence like this, for example, the presence of commas drastically reduces the period's stopping power:

> I went to see the doctor, the one on my corner, just for a quick visit, on my way to work.

But in a sentence like this, the period, as the only form of punctuation, wields supreme power:

> I went to see the doctor on my way to work.

The comma can also take away stopping power from the semicolon and make it feel nearly superfluous:

> It's hard for me to say it, but, after thinking it over all weekend, I realized, without any prodding, that I knew the answer all along, and that it was that I love her, I really do; but that doesn't mean she'll marry me.

But in a sentence like this, the semicolon wields its proper power:

> I love her; but that doesn't mean she'll marry me.

Of course, in the above example the content was also radically changed, and we begin to see that punctuation and content are inherently connected: certain content is not possible with certain punctuation, and certain punctuation lends itself to certain content. For example, it is harder to fill a shorter sentence with commas. Sometimes you will set out to reduce the commas and find yourself altering the content of the sentence itself.

In the above examples, it depends on your intention. If you are more concerned with the impact of the comma than the period or semicolon, keep it. What matters is that your choice is deliberate.

You must also consider stylistic consistency. You always want to offer readers as smooth a ride as possible, and this means you don't want some sentences full of commas and others bereft. You want to establish a style and stick to it as much as possible. Consider:

> We walked into the forest. We hadn't gone far and we'd already lost our way. I knew this would happen. She was wrong again, she always was, and this time I had proof, and I wouldn't let her forget it, especially next time she pretended to be an expert.

You can see how the final sentence, laden with commas while the others are not, stands out, feels jarring in context of the paragraph.

This is an extreme example. More subtle is the comma-to-sentence ratio. Unless you have good reason, you don't want your sentences to randomly jump from two commas to eight commas (assuming they are the same word length and their clauses are approximately the same length). Readers pick up on everything. Uneven comma placement will work on them, and jar them rhythmically.

Of course, once you've mastered this rule, you can break it, and deliberately defy consistency. Indeed, sometimes you'll want to stray from uniformity in order to achieve an effect. For example:

> He thought he could grow an orange tree, and once an idea got into his head, there was no stopping him. He planted it that day, grinning like an idiot in the backyard, craving attention like he always did. God I hated him.

The first two sentences have two commas, while the last has none.

Notice the contrast, and the impact. The lack of commas signal to the reader that the final sentence is unlike the others, and therefore significant. Notice that sentence length is also affected: the number of commas present (or absent) often has a direct bearing on sentence length.

More subtle than the number of commas per sentence is *where* you place commas within a sentence—in other words, the length of your clauses. Some writers have asides or digressions that average few words. Such as:

> I went to the theater, the new one, hoping to find something to distract me.

Other writers indulge their asides or digressions, allowing them to run many words:

> I went to the theater, that elaborate concoction recently erected on my block to the endless annoyance of my neighbors, hoping to find something to distract me.

Either is acceptable, and every sentence will have its own requirements and exceptions. But on the whole, one should become aware of where commas are placed within the sentence and the average size of clauses, and be aware of this placement within the context of the work.

WHAT YOUR USE OF THE COMMA
REVEALS ABOUT YOU

The writer who overuses commas tends to also overuse adjectives and adverbs. He tends to be repetitive, won't be subtle, and often gives too much information. He grasps for multiple word choices instead of one strong choice, and thus the choices he makes won't be strong. His language won't be unique. Commas are also used to qualify, offset, or pause, and the writer who frequently resorts to this tends to be reluctant to take a definitive stance. He will be hesitant. His characters, too, might not take a stand; his plot might be ambiguous. It will be harder for him to deliver dramatic punches when need be, and indeed he is less likely to be dramatic. He is interested in fine distinctions, more so than pacing, and is likely to write an overly long book. He writes with critics in mind, with the fear of being criticized for omission, and is more likely to have a scholarly background (or at least be well read) and to consider *too* many angles. This writer will need to simplify, to take a stronger stance, and to understand that less is more.

There are two types of writers who underuse commas: the first is the unsophisticated writer who has not developed an ear for sentence rhythm. He is unable to hear fine distinctions, and thinks writing is solely about conveying information. He will need to spend time reading classic writers and especially poetry, and train himself to hear the music of language. The second is the sophisticated writer who (like Gertrude Stein) has an aversion to commas and underuses them on purpose. There are numerous writers who rebel against the overuse of punctuation, and more often than not they find a target in the poor comma. The danger for these writers is the rare problem of overestimating the reader. Unless a reader is accustomed to reading twelfth-century clergical texts, he will want at least *some* commas, some pauses laid out for him. There is a need for marks—especially commas—to indicate ebbs and flows, pauses and pitch, division of clauses and meaning. The writer who ignores this is the writer who writes for himself, not with the reader in mind. He will not be a commercial writer, or plot oriented, but prose oriented, interested in nuances of style—but to a fault.

EXERCISES

• Choose a sentence from your work that might be confusing to the reader, or perhaps too open for interpretation. (If you can't find such a sentence, then give your work to outside readers, and ask them to point one out.) Can you add any commas to provide clarity? Can you apply this principle to other sentences throughout your work?

• Choose a section of your work where the pace feels too quick, or too choppy, or where there are a series of short sentences that are not very substantial. (If you are unaware of any such section, give your work to outside readers and ask them to find one.) Can you connect any of these sentences with a comma? Can you apply this principle to other sentences throughout your work?

• Choose a section of your work where the pace is too slow, or feels cumbersome, or where there are a series of long sentences. (If you are unaware of any such section, give your work to outside readers and ask them to find one.) Can you remove any commas? Can you apply this principle to other sentences throughout your work?

• Choose a scene that is pivotal for your characters, perhaps where they exchange crucial dialogue. Pick a revelatory moment, one that needs to be slowed and emphasized as much as possible, where every word counts. Can you add a comma to help emphasize a point that you don't want readers to miss? Can you apply this principle to other scenes throughout your work?

• Choose a page from your work and remove all qualifications or asides, along with their commas. For some writers, who rarely use these, this will have little impact. For others, it will make a tremendous difference. How does it read now? Can you apply this principle to any other sentences throughout your work?

- Begin a new piece of creative writing. Write for an entire page without using a single comma. How does it affect the writing? The story? The character? Can you incorporate any of this into your greater work?

- Begin a new scene between two characters, giving each long stretches of dialogue. Don't allow any commas. How does it affect how they speak? Can you incorporate any of this into your greater work?

- Step 1: Look at one page of your work and count the number of commas per sentence. What is the average? Does the number of commas per sentence vary? Now count the total number of commas per page. What's the comma count? Read the page aloud. Remember how it sounds.

  Step 2: Double the number of commas on the page. Now read it aloud. How does it read? What's the difference?

  Step 3: Remove every comma on the page. Now read it aloud. How does it read? What have you learned from this exercise that can be incorporated into your greater work?

CHAPTER

3

THE
SEMICOLON
(the Bridge)

When a writer is taking pains to write for his reader rather than
to impress him, semicolons can seem like the grammarian's
happiest invention.

—JOHN R. TRIMBLE,
Writing with Style

BETWEEN THE comma and the period you'll find the semicolon.
Pausing more strongly than the comma, yet dividing more weakly
than the period, it is a mediator. The semicolon does not have as
many functions as the comma, yet it has more than the period. As
Eric Partridge says in *You Have a Point There*, "By its very form (;)
[the semicolon] betrays its dual nature: it is both period and
comma." As such, it is best thought of as a bridge between two
worlds.

The primary function of the semicolon is to connect two complete (and thematically similar) sentences, thereby making them
one. But when and how to do that is open to interpretation. The
semicolon has been overused (Virginia Woolf's *To the Lighthouse*)
and questionably used (Herman Melville's *Moby-Dick*) throughout
the centuries, and has been the subject of endless debate.
Compounding the debate is the fact that, grammatically, the semi-

colon is never *necessary*; two short sentences can always coexist without being connected. Artistically, though, the semicolon opens a world of possibilities, and can lend a huge impact. In this sense, it is the punctuation mark best suited for creative writers.

The semicolon is a powerful tool in the writer's arsenal. It is probably the most elegant of all forms of punctuation (it has been dubbed "a compliment from the writer to the reader"), and can offer an excellent solution to balancing sentence length and rhythm. Yet it is often overlooked by writers today. So in this chapter we'll focus on how—and why—to use it. We'll learn what we gain from its presence, and what we lose when we don't invite it to the symphony of punctuation.

HOW TO USE IT

The first thing to realize is that one could always make a case for *not* using a semicolon. As an unnecessary form of punctuation, as the luxury item in the store, we must ask ourselves: why use it at all?

We use the semicolon for the same reason we trade cement floors for marble: cement floors are equally functional but not as elegant, not as aesthetically pleasing as marble. The semicolon elevates punctuation from the utilitarian (from punctuation that works) to the luxurious (to punctuation that transcends). Business memos do not need semicolons; creative writers do.

The semicolon's functions are all essentially creative, and are connected with a writer's sensibility. Some ways to use it:

• To connect two closely related sentences. Sometimes two (or more) sentences are so closely related that you won't want the separation of a period, yet they are also so independent that they need stronger separation than a comma can offer. Consider:

He ran with his shirt over his head. He had forgotten his umbrella once again.

Grammatically, the above is correct. Yet these two thoughts are so closely linked that they don't feel quite right standing on their own. A comma won't do, since they are each complete sentences:

He ran with his shirt over his head, he had forgotten his umbrella once again.

Thus, we need the semicolon:

He ran with his shirt over his head; he had forgotten his umbrella once again.

The semicolon lends an appropriate feeling of connection, while allowing each clause its independence. It functions in a position where both the period and comma cannot. Notice how, by connecting these two sentences with a semicolon, each sentence helps explain the other. "He ran with his shirt over his head" is technically complete and correct, yet is somewhat cryptic on its own. The subsequent sentence brings it to life.

Another example:

The wind knocked over two trees on my block alone. The cleanup would be atrocious.

Once again a comma won't do, as these clauses are too independent:

The wind knocked over two trees on my block alone, the cleanup would be atrocious.

Thus, the semicolon:

> The wind knocked over two trees on my block alone; the cleanup
> would be atrocious.

You'll notice that the first example is grammatically acceptable. Yet
adding a semicolon extends the thought, and allows a richer overall sentence.

• Stylistically, in a paragraph plagued by short sentences, a semicolon can smooth out the choppiness. Commas serve a similar
function, yet sometimes a semicolon is more appropriate, especially if you want clauses to be connected yet independent.
Semicolons can allow shorter, complete thoughts without the
choppiness of a period. Consider:

> She wasn't going to support him anymore. It was time for him to get
> a job. He'd never leave the house otherwise. He'd loaf forever if he
> could. He was born that way. It was thanks to his father. It had taken
> her twenty years to get rid of him. She wouldn't go through that
> again. The son had two years. After that, the locks were changed.

All these short sentences give this paragraph a staccato, childlike
feel. If we add a semicolon or two, though, the problem is solved:

> She wasn't going to support him anymore. It was time for him to get
> a job. He'd never leave the house otherwise; he'd loaf forever if he
> could. He was born that way. It was thanks to his father. It had taken
> her twenty years to get rid of him. She wouldn't go through that
> again. The son had two years; after that, the locks were changed.

This version feels more readable, less stylistically pronounced.

The semicolons have lengthened some sentences and smoothed out the rhythm. They also provide sorely needed variety and contrast: instead of a cluster of only short sentences, they create a mix of long and short sentences, which enables each to stand out.

• Semicolons can enable a longer and more complex thought to exist under one umbrella, thus offering readers the satisfaction of digesting a fuller thought at once. Readers used to have longer attention spans, and it was the norm to write in long, complex sentences. For today's readers, such a style would be tiresome, almost academic. Yet I do believe modern readers have the capacity, even the desire, to digest longer and more complex sentences, as long as they are conceptually and rhythmically sound, and offer the rest stops of semicolons. Mark Twain is known for his use of the semicolon; an example from his short story "The Notorious Jumping Frog of Calaveras County":

I have a lurking suspicion that *Leonidas* W. Smiley is a myth; that my friend never knew such a personage; and that he only conjectured that if I asked old Wheeler about him, it would remind him of his infamous *Jim* Smiley, and he would go to work and bore me to death with some exasperating reminiscence of him as long and as tedious as it should be useless to me.

Using semicolons, Twain is able to convey considerably more material under the umbrella of a single sentence.

• The semicolon can enhance word economy, since its appearance often allows surrounding words to be cut. For example:

She couldn't dance in her favorite hall because it was under construction.

She couldn't dance in her favorite hall; it was under construction.

As John Trimble says in *Writing with Style,* "The semicolon is efficient: it allows you to eliminate most of those conjunctions or prepositions that are obligatory with the comma—words like *whereas, because, for, or, but, while, and.*"

Edgar Allan Poe used the semicolon often and with great skill. Consider this excerpt from his story "The Unparalleled Adventure of One Hans Pfaall":

His feet, of course, could not be seen at all. His hands were enormously large. His hair was gray, and collected into a queue behind. His nose was prodigiously long, crooked, and inflammatory; his eyes full, brilliant, and acute; his chin and cheeks, although wrinkled with age, were broad, puffy, and double; but of ears of any kind there was not a semblance to be discovered upon any portion of his head.

The semicolons here are used well not only sentence to sentence but also in context of the paragraph. Poe begins with complete, simple sentences, using only commas and periods, as he describes the man's feet, hands, and hair. But as he switches to describing the man's face, he switches to semicolons. This is not by chance. The pace increases as he does, as if he's revving up in his description of this man, racing toward a conclusion. It enables us to take in this man's entire face at once, as one grand unit (as opposed to the feet, hands, and hair, which are given their own sentences).

Here's another example, perhaps one of the most famous in literature. This comes from the opening paragraph of Melville's *Moby-Dick*. Melville relied heavily on the semicolon to create *Moby-Dick*, and there has been some debate over whether he used it properly or not. Some of his usages are certainly questionable. But this one is not:

Whenever I find myself growing grim about the mouth; whenever it is a damp, drizzly November in my soul; whenever I find myself involuntarily pausing before coffin warehouses, and bringing up the rear of every funeral I meet; and especially whenever my hypos get such an upper hand of me, that it requires a strong moral principle to prevent me from deliberately stepping into the street, and methodically knocking people's hats off—then, I account it high time to get to sea as soon as I can.

This single sentence encapsulates the entire rationale behind the book, behind "Ishmael's" taking the adventure he does. Although it's technically not advisable, Melville could have used commas here, but if he had, the pauses would not have been as long, and the reader wouldn't have had the opportunity to digest each thought. Or he could have, alternately, used periods; but doing so would have made the reader pause *too* long, and not digest all of this as a single idea. Semicolons allowed the reader to pause and also created tension, capturing "Ishmael's" own tension, his own feeling of building restlessness and need to get on board a ship.

"Sometimes you get a glimpse of a semicolon coming, a few lines farther on, and it is like climbing a steep path through woods and seeing a wooden bench just at a bend in the road ahead, a place where you can expect to sit for a moment, catching your breath."
—LEWIS THOMAS

DANGER OF OVERUSE AND MISUSE

The semicolon tends to be underused because many writers don't know how to use it well. They have some notion of its function, but not an exact idea, and when they take their first tentative steps toward using it, they tend to do so incorrectly. Compounding the problem is that placement of the semicolon, like the comma, is somewhat up for debate, and in many circumstances one could just as easily argue for its omission.

There are, however, some instances when the semicolon is clearly misused. The most common:

• The semicolon should never be used to link two sentences unless they are closely related. For example, this could work:

> The police station was close to his house; he would have to be careful.

But this could not:

> The police station was close to his house; he needed to do his laundry soon.

When using a semicolon, you must always ask yourself if the two sentences are closely linked. If not, omit the semicolon. Even if two sentences are related, in most cases it's preferable *not* to link them with a semicolon. Sometimes thoughts need to stand on their own, and are better digested separately. This is especially true if the reader needs time to ponder each thought.

• Sometimes sentences linked by semicolons are *too* closely related—in other words, sometimes a semicolon is used when merely a comma will do. For example, this sentence:

The gardeners worked all day; their machines blared all the time.

should more likely be:

The gardeners worked all day, their machines blaring all the time.

There is no question a pause is needed between these two clauses—the issue is how strong that pause needs to be. In this case, the clauses are too closely linked and it's the comma's job (which also mandates minor word changes). This especially holds true when dealing with a series of short sentences.

• In most cases, avoid linking two longer (or independent) sentences with a semicolon. The semicolon allows a fuller, more complex thought, but when that thought is already full (or independent), you can overburden it by tacking on yet another thought. Periods serve their function well, which is to allow separation between thoughts. You don't want a semicolon to break down that barrier unless there is an important reason for doing so. For example, here are two complete sentences:

My neighbor's fence was purple and hideous and fell apart every winter, encroaching on my property. She had built it with her own hands, she constantly reminded me.

These two sentences each convey a lot on their own, and should not be connected, as they are here:

My neighbor's fence was purple and hideous and fell apart every winter, encroaching on my property; she had built it with her own hands, she constantly reminded me.

This overwhelms the reader. Although technically this works, in reality it makes the single thought too cumbersome for most readers, makes it harder to fully digest each idea. Sometimes separation is warranted.

• Once you get into the semicolon habit, it can become too easy to link everything: you can become a semicolon junkie. There is a real danger of becoming too trigger happy with semicolons, of inserting them when not truly needed. Given the fact that nearly any two (related) complete sentences can be linked, the potential for using semicolons is limitless. Once a writer starts to use the semicolon regularly, it can become hard to stop, and he may never look at a pair of sentences the same way again. Consider:

> The telephone wire was down again; the phone company had told me it would be up by this morning; once again, bad information; I wouldn't let them get away with it this time.

Linking like this allows you to get away with half thoughts—instead of fully developing a single thought—and can overwhelm the style of a text. You must remember that periods and commas serve their function well.

The other problem with overusing semicolons is that it can create a work that feels overly formal. The semicolon is a rather sophisticated punctuation mark and if overdone it will feel as if you're showing off, or being elitist. "Good stylists try to avoid [the semicolon] as too formal: decked out, as it were, in a starched shirt and a black suit," says Rene J. Cappon says in *The Associated Press Guide to Punctuation*. That doesn't mean it can't be used—it just should be reserved for the right occasion.

• Sentences have beginnings, middles, and ends. When semicolons are overused, the natural arc and rhythm of a sentence can be lost. For example, this sentence stands well on its own:

The sun lit up the wall, and I shielded my eyes from the glare.

But if you connect it with semicolons:

The sun lit up the wall; I shielded my eyes from the glare.

While acceptable, it isn't quite as smooth. It feels more like one divided thought than two distinct thoughts. Neither clause feels as if it naturally rises and falls.

• Periods are effective at creating a bang, especially at the end of short sentences. Semicolons, though, rarely can, since they don't offer a full stop. And sometimes this "bang" effect is needed. For example, here we don't feel the impact of the final sentence:

The bus let me off at the wrong stop for the third time that week; it won't happen again.

But when we take away the semicolon:

The bus let me off at the wrong stop for the third time that week. It won't happen again.

We now feel the desired effect. As you can see, in the former example, the semicolon actually detracted from the punch.

> "I have been told that the dying words of one famous
> 20th century writer were, 'I should have used fewer
> semicolons.'"
>
> —LYNNE TRUSS, *Eats, Shoots & Leaves*

CONTEXT

More so than any punctuation mark, the semicolon is designed to help the surrounding punctuation. It is the ultimate team player, its very existence relative to others. Thus context must always be carefully considered when employing the semicolon. A few circumstances to consider:

- A semicolon can be called in when a comma is not enough. There are times when a comma is already used too much in one sentence, when it can't do its job effectively anymore. There are also times when multiple thoughts in a sentence need more separation than merely a comma, need more time and space to be digested. But a period is sometimes too strong, provides too much separation. The semicolon can step in and save the day, allow a more substantial pause while not severing thoughts completely. For example, Washington Irving used the semicolon heavily and well in his story "Rip Van Winkle":

In fact, he declared it was of no use to work on his farm; it was the most pestilent little piece of ground in the whole country; everything about it went wrong, and would go wrong, in spite of him. His fences were continually falling to pieces; his cow would either go astray, or get among the cabbages; weeds were sure to grow quicker in his fields than anywhere else; the rain always made a point of setting in just as he had some out-door work to do; so that though his patrimonial estate had dwindled away under his management, acre by acre, until there was little more left than a mere patch of Indian corn and potatoes, yet it was the worst conditioned farm in the neighborhood.

Notice how using the semicolon enables the reader to take in such a long, full image, yet at the same time allows the reader some time to pause between these images, allows more breathing room than if there had merely been commas. Thanks to the semicolons, we can take in the image of the decrepit condition of his farm at once, making its impact all the more powerful.

• The semicolon can provide clarity in a sentence plagued by commas. When too many commas are on the scene, a sentence can become confusing; a semicolon can step in and divide the clauses, bringing clarity back to the sentence. As Lynne Truss says in *Eats, Shoots & Leaves*, the semicolon "performs the duties of a kind of Special Policeman in the event of comma fights." Consider:

I wanted the shovel and the rake, the pitchfork she could keep.

I wanted the shovel and the rake; the pitchfork she could keep.

In the former example, it is hard to tell where one thought ends and another begins, while in the latter it's clear.

• Sometimes a period needs the help of a semicolon, too. There comes a point when a period loses its effectiveness, when a series of short sentences simply can't bear another one. A comma won't always be able to help, especially if there are numerous self-contained sentences. Consider:

The barbecue was going fine until my father-in-law arrived. Within five minutes he was telling me how to cook. When to flip. What kind of meat to use. I could kill him.

There are too many periods here, giving the text a choppy feel (unless the author is trying to create an extremely stylized text). Commas could be brought in, but they wouldn't provide long enough pauses to hammer each point home. Thus, the semicolon:

The barbecue was going fine until my father-in-law arrived. Within five minutes he was telling me how to cook; when to flip; what kind of meat to use. I could kill him.

The semicolon not only nicely connects these short sentences, but also allows the last sentence to stand out from the others. The period is able to take a long, well-deserved rest, and then once again exert its power.

Using a semicolon before a period, particularly in a longer sentence, can also help restore the bang to the period. For example:

You may well ask why I write. And yet my reasons are quite many. For it is not unusual in human beings who have witnessed the sack of a city or the falling to pieces of a people to desire to set down what they have witnessed for the benefit of unknown heirs or of generations infinitely remote; or, if you please, just to get the sight out of their heads.

This comes from Ford Madox Ford's novel *The Good Soldier*. By placing the semicolon where he does, we feel the impact of the final period, an impact we would not have felt otherwise. Notice also the wonderful contrast between the long clause preceding the semicolon and the short one following it, which makes each stand out. Notice also how he varies his punctuation throughout, beginning with two short sentences, and avoiding commas in the first part of the third sentence. Each of these choices mirrors the intent of the content.

• Taking a step back and looking at a paragraph in context, it's easier to see the flaws. Some sentences will be too long, some too short, and some long-short combinations will be jarring. The semicolon is the great balancer. There is no better tool to help smooth out a group of sentences and allow them to work within the context of the paragraph. Consider this example from F. Scott Fitzgerald's *Tender Is the Night:*

> Before eight a man came down to the beach in a blue bathrobe and with much preliminary application to his person of the chilly water, and much grunting and loud breathing, floundered a minute in the sea. When he had gone, beach and bay were quiet for an hour. Merchantmen crawled westward on the horizon; bus boys shouted in the hotel court; the dew dried upon the pines.

The punctuation in each of these sentences mirrors the content. The opening, long sentence, captures the feeling of the man spending a long time at the beach. The second, short sentence captures the peace and quiet after he leaves. And the final sentence prolongs that quiet, captures what it means in particular. Note also how, in context, the semicolon balances the paragraph. If the final sentence had been broken up with periods (making three short sentences), the paragraph would have been too choppy.

• Keep in mind that a semicolon takes the pause effect away from a nearby comma, and takes the stop effect away from a nearby period. When the semicolon connects, the comma becomes less important; when it divides, the period seems less meaningful. Commas and periods do have a power of their own. Their effect can be lost when too many (or ill-placed) semicolons come onto the scene. And there might be times when you want the impact to fall on the comma or period. Even though the semicolon can work in any given circumstance, it doesn't mean it should. Always be mindful of its stealing the limelight.

Alternately, sometimes you can use the semicolon to actually enhance the power of a comma or period. By creating a long sentence with a semicolon, for example, you give yourself the opportunity to contrast it with a shorter sentence. Consider this example from Harold Brodkey's *Profane Friendship*:

> Here is the self and the hovering moment; here is the trembling, nervous, seemingly near motionlessness of the surface of the water; here is the rustling bowwave and wake; here they are in subduedly echoing canals in Murano; then here is the Lagoon again, Venice ahead obscured; here is *San Michele* on the left pretending that the dead are silent and are not numberless; here is the gouging and choppy passage of the white motorboat over gray fluidities, the lighted grayish rain-teased air holding a glow as of a decomposing moon, and I am enveloped in flitters of memory which I resist of the canals in Venice itself, the wrinkled water in the *rio* behind our house, the secret hushes and whispers there, time's indescribable motion on a Venetian afternoon. I was a child here. And here is my history of love.

He offers his observations of Italy as he flies over it, and the semicolons here allow us to absorb an (extremely) full image at once. They offer a nice parallel to the content itself, since flying over a country would, indeed, offer several images at once, yet with a bit of separation. But notice especially how Brodkey concludes this excerpt, the radical brevity of the final two sentences. It is a supreme example of context, of radically contrasting sentence length in order to make a point stand out.

WHAT YOUR USE OF THE SEMICOLON REVEALS ABOUT YOU

As the semicolon is an advanced tool, the writer who overuses it is likely to be somewhat advanced, one who takes chances with language and strives to make it the best it can be. This bodes well. However, since the semicolon is also a fairly formal, classy tool, the writer who overuses it is also likely to lean toward pretentiousness. He is more likely to write in flowery, ornate prose, and the writing is likely to be overly intricate. Simplification is needed. This writer is likely to be more prose than plot oriented, and will suffer from a slower pace and less action. His writing will more likely lack a dramatic punch.

It is hard to underuse the semicolon, since a work can exist perfectly well without one. That said, there are cases when it is called for, and the writer who completely ignores it is likely to either be a beginner, or hesitant to take chances with language. He is less likely to have well-crafted prose, less likely to offer nuances of style and language. The good news, at least, is that he writes with simplicity, which bodes well for clarity of thought and will serve him well once he masters his craft. He is also likely to offer a quicker pace.

EXERCISES

- Count the number of semicolons on the first page of one of your works. Now count the total number in your first chapter. What's the semicolon count per page? Per chapter? Do you barely use them? Or use them abundantly? Awareness is the first step.

• Look for a place in your work that contains a cluster of short sentences that are related to each other. Can you connect any of these with a semicolon? What effect does it have? Can you apply this technique elsewhere in your work?

• Look for a place in your work that contains several longer sentences that need to be long since they contain one or more complex thoughts. Can you break up any of these sentences with a semicolon? What effect does it have? Can you apply this technique elsewhere in your work?

• Look for a place in your work where you use an abundance of semicolons. Can you cut some of them? What effect does it have? Can you apply this technique elsewhere in your work? (Notice how deleting semicolons gives power back to commas and periods.)

• Look for a place in your work that reads too fast, where you'd like to slow the pace. Can you combine any sentences using semicolons? What effect does it have on pacing? Can you apply this technique elsewhere in your work?

• Look for a place in your work that you feel reads too slowly, where you'd like to speed up the pace. Can you delete any semicolons? What effect does it have on pacing? Can you apply this technique elsewhere in your work?

• Look for a paragraph in your work that contains sentences of wildly varying length. Can you use a semicolon to balance out sentence length? What effect does it have? Can you apply this technique elsewhere in your work?

Part 2

INTO THE LIMELIGHT

(the colon, dash, parentheses, quotation marks, paragraph and section breaks)

If you think that you can write an even passable letter without knowing how to use one and preferably two other stops (comma and semicolon), you are making a grave mistake. To go further: if you think you can write a good business report or an essay or an article, without knowing also how to employ at least two of the remaining stops—the colon, the dash, and parentheses—then you are probably over-estimating your own abilities as a writer and the intelligence of your readers.

—ERIC PARTRIDGE,
You Have a Point There

While the punctuation marks discussed in part 1 (the period, comma, and semicolon) are the construction team of the punctuation world, the types of punctuation we'll cover in part 2 (the colon, dash, parentheses, quotation marks, paragraph and section breaks) exist to add flair. This is not to say that these marks don't also effect sentence construction—they can and certainly do. But, their most distinctive feature is their ability to make words stand out.

They have the unique ability to propel words or clauses into the limelight, and their appearance always carry with them a good deal of panache. They are the drama queens of the punctuation world.

Additionally, with the exception of the paragraph break, these marks rarely appear because they need to—they appear only if they *want* to. In fact, technically one could write a book without ever using one of these marks. The word "utilitarian" does not exist in their vocabulary. Fittingly, this part of the book will take the reader beyond the utilitarian and into the world of rarefied writing. Our house has been built. Now it's time to add the detail.

THE COLON

(the Magician)

What is one man's colon is another man's comma.

—MARK TWAIN

THE COLON is the magician of the punctuation world. It holds its audience in suspense, waits until just the right moment, then voilà: it pulls back the curtain to reveal the result. It sits on the very peak of drama, with all that comes before building to it, and all that follows a denouement. As such, it is one of the most effective punctuation marks to propel a word or clause into the limelight. (This is why the colon comes first in this section of the book.) Indeed, it is impossible to follow a colon in an inconspicuous way.

Like the semicolon, the colon tends to be underused by creative writers, and when used, not used well. Most writers seem intimidated to use it creatively, perhaps because they equate it with its mundane usages (such as heralding a list, or a letter, or separating minutes from seconds on a clock). Other writers use it once or twice but find themselves overwhelmed by its dramatic power and are unsure where to go from there. The avoidance of the colon is unfortunate, since it is one of the most powerful tools in the arsenal of a creative writer.

HOW TO USE IT

• In its most majestic, overt form the colon reveals. Indeed, when it comes to dramatic revelation, the colon has no second. In this function, the colon acts as a mark point, with the text preceding it building to a revelation, and the text that follows living up to the promise. The highly visual colon helps us immediately distinguish two parts of the sentence, to know that we are crossing a threshold. Consider:

> I grabbed my bag, put on my coat, and stepped out the door, as I wasn't coming back.

In this example, we don't feel a revelation, don't feel the impact of "I wasn't coming back." Adding a colon, though, changes everything:

> I grabbed my bag, put on my coat, and stepped out the door: I wasn't coming back.

Now we know this is a peak moment; now the sentence is divided neatly into parts, and there is a clear purpose for each. The colon has shown us that the focus of this sentence is not the bag, the coat, or the stepping out, but the fact that he wasn't coming back. It has propelled this clause into the limelight.

Keep in mind that in order to achieve this, you must first craft a sentence where the opening clause builds to a revelation and the second portion delivers. A revelation is ineffective without preparation, and preparation is pointless without revelation.

• The colon can be used, simply, to offset a point. Sometimes a point, like a youngest child, needs to stand out, to be given extra attention, perhaps for clarity's sake, or for fear of its getting lost in the midst of a complex sentence. You must always consider whether the sleepy, 2:00 a.m. reader might accidentally gloss over a word or clause. If this is your intention (as it is for some writers who strive to be subtle), then that is fine, but if not, you must think of the reader, and assume the worst-case scenario. Reading is a different experience for everyone, and if an idea is important enough that you can't afford to take the chance of its being missed, a colon will make sure it stands out. With a colon present, the first part of the sentence will be the equivalent of, "I have a point to make, are you ready?" and then the point will follow. Compare this:

The engineer couldn't climb the telephone pole because he was scared of heights.

With this:

The engineer couldn't climb the telephone pole: he was scared of heights.

In the first example, "he was scared of heights" might not have full impact. In the second example, with the colon, it cannot possibly be missed.

• The colon can be used to enhance word economy. A writer must embrace any device that helps create a tighter, more economical work, and a colon allows you to eliminate words such as "that is," "namely," and "because."

I've been meaning to tell you something, and that is that I'm pregnant.

I've been meaning to tell you something: I'm pregnant.

I didn't want to leave her alone for Christmas because her friend had just died.

I didn't want to leave her alone for Christmas: her friend had just died.

• The colon can be used to summarize. If you're describing the attributes of a character, or the elements of a house, or the methodology of a prison, and you want to take your observations and summarize them in one grand impression, the colon can do the job. Consider:

> The parlor was immense, the kitchen spectacular, the two billiard rooms offered a water view and the six fireplaces were always lit: it was a palace.

In this capacity, the colon allows you to take a sentence one step further, to take your observations and parlay them into an impression. You could summarize without using a colon, but then it wouldn't necessarily be clear to the reader that the impression is the direct conclusion of all that came before. There are instances where one might want a conclusion to be distinct from the observations that preceded it; but there are also times when you need it all clearly tied together.

Along these lines, the colon can be used not only to summarize in the strict sense, but also to elucidate, to elaborate on the text that preceded it. Consider this example from Alice Walker's story "Everyday Use":

> Maggie will be nervous until after her sister goes: she will stand hopelessly in corners, homely and ashamed of the burn scars down her arms and legs, eying her sister with a mixture of envy and awe.

All of the text that follows the colon is an elucidation on what it means for Maggie to be "nervous." A lesser writer would have separated these ideas with a period. By using the colon, Walker keeps all of the images connected to the idea of being "nervous," elaborates on what that really means.

• The colon can be used to herald a list. This is often a mundane usage of the colon, but in the hands of a great creative writer, it can be transformed into an artful usage. Amy Tan, for example, uses it well in her story "Two Kinds":

> America was where all my mother's hopes lay. She had come here in 1949 after losing everything in China: her mother and father, her family home, her first husband, and two daughters, twin baby girls.

The "items" in this list are not items at all, but each an incredibly powerful image, an incredibly powerful loss. By listing them like this, Tan plays against the grain of the standard usage of the colon, rattling off losses as if they are common items, and showing us the strength of the narrator's mother, who has survived so much more than we could possibly imagine, but who has compartmentalized.

> Now facing the flaming sky in the west, and now facing the sharp mountains, the car followed the dusty trail down the canyons into air which began to smell of other things besides the endless ozone of the heights: orange blossoms, pepper, sun-baked excrement, burning olive oil, rotten fruit.

This comes from Paul Bowles's story "A Distant Episode." Most writers would have merely listed one or two items to convey a sense of smell; by choosing to list so many, and to use a colon to herald them, Bowles wants us to slow down, to really take in the place.

• The colon can be used to pause. Periods and semicolons provide a pause between thoughts, commas provide a pause between clauses, but no other punctuation mark can provide a substantial pause *within* the same thought. The pause created by the colon is useful for all of the colon's functions: it preps the stage for a dramatic revelation, for a summary, or for a conclusion. It gives us a slight feeling of separation, a bit of breathing room to prepare for the finale. Even the spacing required around a colon points to its ability to create separation: in the past, two spaces were required after the colon (as opposed to the mere one space required after a comma and semicolon), and hundreds of years ago, the colon was the only punctuation mark to require two spaces after it *and two spaces before it.*

Sometimes a pause is necessary within the same sentence to allow something to sink in. Consider:

I want to tell you that I love you.

We don't feel a pause here, or a revelation. But if we add a colon:

I want to tell you something: I love you.

Now there is just enough of a pause to give the words impact. By adding the colon (and modifying the surrounding words accordingly) we've also created an arc to the sentence, a sense of building and of resolution.

• Just as the colon can be used to create a feeling of summary within a sentence, so can the colon, in the greatest context, be used for finality at the end of a section, chapter, or book. This is a device to be used sparingly, since the conclusion of a chapter or book is inherently dramatic, and mustn't be overdone. But when one needs a grand final sentence, sometimes only a colon will do. For example, consider this conclusion:

> As they stood on the ice and watched the huge ship steam away they felt their sudden isolation, and it dawned on them that there was no turning back, that it would be a long, hard winter.

Somehow this doesn't feel as final as it could. But with a colon:

> As they stood on the ice and watched the huge ship steam away they felt their sudden isolation, and it dawned on them that there was no turning back: it would be a long, hard winter.

The finality is unmistakable. The colon here is like the final drumbeat at the end of a song, like the "The End" title card that appears after the film credits have rolled. Again, in most cases a final colon would be overkill, and it is preferable to construct the final sentence in a way where the finality is inherent, and not reliant upon a colon to do its job. Nonetheless, sometimes nothing else will work, and for this sort of job, the colon has no equal.

Let's look at some examples from literature. George Bernard Shaw was famous for his use of the colon. He relied on it heavily. Many of his usages are questionable—in fact, overall, I don't think he used it well. Nonetheless, here is an interesting example from his play *Widowers' Houses*. It is especially interesting because he manages to squeeze two colons into one sentence:

> The other, Mr. William de Burgh Cokane, is probably over 40, possibly 50: an ill-nourished, scanty-haired gentleman, with affected manners: fidgety, touchy, and constitutionally ridiculous in uncompassionate eyes.

A colon can work well in summing up a character, particularly after listing his attributes, and here Shaw states Mr. Cokane's age, then uses a colon to go deeper into what it means to be that age. He segues to the man's manners, then uses another colon to go deeper into precisely how these manners manifest. With Shaw, each colon is like a "zoom in" button: he touches on something, then uses a colon to bring us to the next level.

Here is an example from James Joyce's short story "The Boarding House," suggested by critically acclaimed author and writing teacher Ellen Cooney:

> For her only one reparation could make up for the loss of her daughter's honour: marriage.

Notice how Joyce uses nearly the entire sentence to build to the colon, and simply a one-word revelation in its wake. The contrast is magnificent. It puts the word "marriage" in the strongest possible spotlight.

> I walked close to the left wall when I entered, but it was empty: just the stairs curving up into shadows.

This is from William Faulkner's *The Sound and the Fury*. Faulkner could have used a period and broken this into two separate sentences, or used a dash to indicate an afterthought. But he chose to use a colon. By doing so, he intimates that the "stairs curving up into shadows" are an enhancement of what it means to be "empty." It is a terrifically melancholy image, and brings home to the reader the experience of emptiness.

Here's an example from the opening of Alice Munro's story "Royal Beatings":

Royal beating. That was Flo's promise. You are going to get one Royal Beating.

The word Royal lolled on Flo's tongue, took on trappings. Rose had a need to picture things, to pursue absurdities, that was stronger than the need to stay out of trouble, and instead of taking this threat to heart she pondered: how is a beating royal?

The colon here makes us pause, makes us feel her "pondering." It also sets us up for the question she asks herself, and for her unexpected viewpoint. Note also Munro's use of other punctuation marks here: she begins by using the period heavily, with three short sentences, followed by an immediate paragraph break. Then she brings in the comma, and her sentences grow longer, culminating in her incredibly long, final sentence, a colon, then a final question mark. This varied punctuation makes us feel the impact of the colon all the more, especially since the portion of the text that precedes it is so long compared to the portion that follows it.

"When we are very young, we tend to regard the ability to use a colon much as a budding pianist regards the ability to play with crossed hands: many of us, when we are older, regard it as a proof of literary skill, maturity, even of sophistication: and many, whether young, not so young, or old, employ it gauchely, haphazardly or, at best, inconsistently."

—ERIC PARTRIDGE, *You Have a Point There*

DANGER OF OVERUSE OR MISUSE

You can get away with a work devoid of colons, but if you misuse or overuse them, it will stand out, and readers will be unforgiving. Like semicolons, colons are addictive. A colon gives a writer an anchor, helps him construct a sentence—indeed, an entire thought. It enables the writer to *think* differently, in rising and falling arcs, with soaring openings and neat conclusions. But not every sentence is meant to progress in such an arc. For the reader, sentence after colon-laden sentence is like riding in a sea with endless rolling waves: he will grow seasick and want off the boat. Consider:

> He went to the park every day to do one thing: feed the pigeons. He loved those damned birds more than he loved me, and I'd had enough: it was time to move out. I packed my bags, left him a note, and put it in the one place he wouldn't miss it: on his bag of bird feed.

Colons are stylistic, and demand the text around them to be stylized. Use them sparingly. If more than one or two appear per page you are probably overdoing it and should find a way to reduce them or, preferably, reconstruct your sentences in a way where the arc is inherent.

• Sometimes a colon is not truly necessary. A colon should connect two clauses only when such connection is crucial, for instance, when one clause reveals or summarizes the other. If the text after a colon reveals, then the text preceding it must build to that revelation. The clauses cannot be unrelated, or too independent. If so, they must be divided into two separate sentences. And that's the job of the period. For example, this cannot work:

My grandfather shot squirrels in his spare time: I didn't do my homework yesterday.

These two clauses are not related, and thus a colon cannot be used. In order to use a colon, the text would need to read something like this:

My grandfather shot squirrels in his spare time: he loved to kill anything that moved.

Similarly, two clauses might be vaguely related to one another, yet not make a perfect match, not truly summarize or reveal each other. Like this:

The lightbulb died while I was drinking my coffee: this coffee tastes horrible.

This sentence should either be reconstructed to make the two clauses a better match, like this:

The lightbulb died while I was drinking my coffee: the electricity in this building is awful.

Or be reconstructed without a colon, like this:

The lightbulb died while I was drinking my coffee. This coffee tastes horrible.

If the connection between two clauses isn't perfect, then a colon should not be present.

• Conversely, relying too heavily on the colon can lead you to create half sentences, form half thoughts, where the first clause of the sentence cannot be completed without the second, and the second clause cannot exist without the first. While the two clauses must be connected and relevant to each other, at the same time you cannot allow this to be an excuse to write flimsy, half clauses that cannot exist without their colon counterparts. The colon strengthens the sentence as a whole, yet it weakens the individual parts, as they can no longer exist without each other. Consider:

> I went to the movies on Tuesday afternoons: that was when tickets were half price.

Technically, the first portion of this sentence could stand on its own, but it would be hard to make a case that the second portion could (unless the writing is stylized), and even the first portion would make a weak sentence. Ultimately, the two clauses of this sentence need each other to allow a full thought. You can get away with this from time to time, but if you rely heavily on this sort of construction, your sentences will become too dependent on the colon. As a rule, the text preceding and following a colon must be more independent than text demarcated by a comma, yet less independent than text demarcated by a semicolon. For example, this sentence could exist without a colon if need be:

> I went to the movies on Tuesday afternoons, since that was when tickets were half price.

Remember, only use a colon if you must.

• As with all punctuation, the need to use the colon must be organic to the text. If a colon is forced onto a sentence—for example, in order to try to force drama where there is none—then that colon will feel fake, and readers will resent it. A colon must never be forced to do the job of content. If a sentence is inherently dramatic, often a colon won't be needed; and when it is needed, it must flow seamlessly into the rhythm of the sentence. The more subtle the better, especially when it comes to the colon. It is such an inherently dramatic, attention-grabbing tool, that one must always tone it down. Forcing a colon into a sentence is like blasting a fog horn while waiting at a stop sign.

Here the colon is forced, making the sentence feel cheap:

The drums rolled, the curtain rose, and there she stood, in the spotlight: my favorite actress.

With the colon removed and some rearranging, it reads more naturally:

The drums rolled, the curtain rose, and there, in the spotlight, stood my favorite actress.

It is an inherently dramatic sentence; "my favorite actress" will shine either way. Using the colon is overkill.

"To be mulcted of our money and mutilated of our property is serious enough: to be deprived of our colon would be intolerable."
—ERIC PARTRIDGE, *You Have a Point There*

CONTEXT

Although the colon may be bossy, it is also sensitive: the punctuation surrounding it has great effect upon it. Likewise, it also has great effect upon other marks. There are many issues to consider when it comes to using the colon in context:

• In order to get maximum effect out of a colon, the text that precedes it should ideally be unimpeded by other punctuation, while the text that follows should flow unimpeded to the sentence's end. When no other punctuation marks exist, the text can race headlong into a colon and then race to a conclusion. The colon becomes the star player, shining by itself in the midst of the sentence. Of course, it needn't always be this way, and there are many fine examples of colons functioning well while commas and semicolons abound on either side. But this will maximize the colon's effect. Consider:

> Halogen lamps, left on at night, can be dangerous, if not deadly: many fires have started as a direct result of their overheating.

The commas in this sentence detract from the impact of the colon. If we remove them, though, and keep just the colon, we can feel the difference:

> Halogen lamps left on at night can be dangerous if not deadly: many fires have started as a direct result of their overheating.

If we go one step further and remove not just the commas but the clauses they contain, we can even more powerfully feel the colon's impact:

Halogen lamps can be deadly: many fires have started as a direct result of their overheating.

This example is more streamlined. The colon can shine here. We feel the sentence rush toward the moment of revelation, then rush to its conclusion.

As you can see, the colon, when used properly, tends to muscle other punctuation out of the way. When using it, beware: it will minimize your use of surrounding punctuation, or at the very least, swallow up their effect. It is the fighting fish in the tank of dociles, and eventually it will be the only fish left. The colon even detracts from the power of the period. For a period to have maximum power, readers shouldn't be slowed at any point throughout the sentence, and the colon slows them in a major way. With a near full stop before the final stop, the final stop is no longer so important. Consider:

Every time I try to speak she does it again: she interrupts me.

The major stop in the rhythm come after "again," thus detracting from the stopping power of the period. But if we remove the colon (and trim the sentence accordingly), then the period's power can be felt again:

Every time I try to speak she interrupts me.

The colon doesn't play well with semicolons either. A semicolon is a semi-full stop and implies it is the penultimate stop before the period. Theoretically a colon could follow a semicolon, but more often than not it would read awkwardly. There is rarely room for both of these giants in the universe of one sentence.

There are always exceptions, though, particularly in the hands of a master author. In the following example from *The Autobiography of My Mother*, Jamaica Kincaid breaks the rules skillfully:

> When my mother died, leaving me a small child vulnerable to all the world, my father took me and placed me in the care of the same woman he paid to wash his clothes. It is possible that he emphasized to her difference between the two bundles: one was his child, not his only child in the world but the only child he had with the only woman he had married so far; the other was his soiled clothes.

The colon here is a powerful choice, setting the stage to elaborate on the "difference" between the two "bundles" of clothing. And the semicolon, surprisingly, works well with it, forcing us to a stop right before the end of the sentence, and allowing a pithy contrast.

• The primary function of the colon is to flag something as important, whether it's a revelation, summary, conclusion, or a point that needs to be offset. The colon is a giant red flag. And if you flag every point as important, readers will stop taking it seriously. Imagine looking at two documents, one with dozens of red flags and the other with merely one. In the former, with everything marked as important, nothing will seem to be; in the latter, the one flagged point will be spotted immediately. It's all about context. When you overuse it, the colon loses its effect. Revelations will no longer have any import. To keep the colon strong, keep context in mind, and use it sparingly.

An example of a skillful (and unusual) placement of a colon in context of a paragraph comes from the opening of Jonathan Franzen's *The Corrections:*

The madness of an autumn prairie cold front coming through. You could feel it: something terrible was going to happen. The sun low in the sky, a minor light, a cooling star. Gust after gust of disorder. Trees restless, temperatures falling, the whole northern religion of things coming to an end. No children in the yards here.

While the colon is normally used to culminate, Franzen goes against the grain and uses it here to *open* his novel. At first it might feel jarring, but as you read on, you realize it works well; instead of summarizing a paragraph, it sets the stage for one. With every sentence we read in its wake, we keep in the back of our minds that something terrible is going to happen. Note also the heavy use of the period here, the numerous short, incomplete sentences. The style is skillfully established within a few moments of the novel's opening.

WHAT YOUR USE OF THE COLON
REVEALS ABOUT YOU

As with other punctuation marks, how you use (or don't use) the colon reveals a lot about you as a writer.

The overuse of the colon generally indicates an overly dramatic writer. This writer's primary concern is making a bang, slamming the reader with a revelation. His greater plot might likewise offer cheap revelations, shocking plot twists, uncovered secrets, surprise endings. Just as the writer who overuses the colon forces drama on a sentence to sentence basis, so will he likely employ more flash than substance. He is more likely to have a cat jump out and scare you than a long, slow build to genuine terror. He wants immediate gratification, and quick fixes.

Since the colon can be used to neatly summarize or conclude, the overuse of the colon can indicate the writer who likes to tie things into neat packages—not just on a sentence-to-sentence basis, but in the greater plot as well. His subplots might tie together too perfectly, his characters might journey through the too-perfect arc—he might even offer moral lessons to be learned. This writer is more inclined to write for the sum of all parts than for the parts themselves. He might be uncomfortable with morally ambiguous characters, and he will more likely people his work with straightforward good and evil characters.

The good news for this writer is that overuse bodes better than underuse. The writer who uses the colon at least has the reader in mind: he's trying to please, whether by offering a revelation, or a neat summary. And since the colon is fairly unusual, its overuse indicates a writer who grapples with the craft, who is interested in bettering his writing and in using every tool at his disposal. Assuming it is used properly, it indicates at least a slight level of sophistication, since the amateur is highly unlikely to overuse the colon, or indeed to use it at all.

Which brings us to the underuse (or absence) of the colon. The colon is a mark that never truly needs to appear in a work, and thus it is hard to criticize a text bereft of them. Nonetheless, there will inevitably be at least a few instances when a colon can be used to enhance, and thus its absence (when needed) might indicate a writer who, at the most basic level is less seasoned, unable or unwilling to experiment with nuances. He is also less likely to use other sophisticated marks, such as semicolons.

While the chronic user of the colon will be overly dramatic, the under-user will likely lack drama. He is likely a realist, creating reality-based characters and reality-based plots that are very accurate—yet also boring. Drama is not his main objective, and the writing may suffer for it. This is not a writer of revelations, nor is it one of tidy summary or conclusions. His characters are more likely to be ambiguous, and not in a satisfying way. Endings are likely to be less satisfying. This is not the sum-of-all-parts writer: this writer writes for the parts themselves.

EXERCISES

Most writers are more likely to underuse the colon, or not use it at all. Thus in order to allow you to become comfortable with it, let's get acquainted with using the colon in all its forms. Practice using the colon:

• For a dramatic revelation. Find a moment in one of your works where you need to drop a bombshell, and yet it doesn't come across as strongly as it should. Incorporate a colon at the crucial moment. What difference does it make? Do you feel the revelation? Can you apply this technique elsewhere in your work?

• For summation. Choose a place in one of your works where you describe something at length and would like to conclude with an overall impression. Perhaps it's a passage where you describe a character or setting. As you conclude your description, use a colon at just the right moment. What difference does it make? Can you apply this technique elsewhere in your work?

• For a conclusion. While concluding a paragraph, section, chapter, or book with a colon can be heavy handed, sometimes it is needed. See if you can find a moment that concludes without the proper finality. Can you add a colon? What difference does it make? Can you apply this technique elsewhere in your work?

• For those of you who may, conversely, use too many colons, start with a colon count. How many colons appear on the first page? On every page in the first chapter? What is the average number of colons per page? If more than two, cut back. Of course, that's only a first step. You must also ask yourself why you overused them to begin with. Are you writing in an overly dramatic way? Are you relying on punctuation to take the place of content?

• Take a close look at the instances when you do use a colon. Is it always truly necessary? Do the two halves of the sentence truly depend on each other? Does one build and the other reveal, or conclude? If not, remove the colon, or reconstruct the sentences so that each portion inherently feeds off the other.

THE DASH AND PARENTHESES

(the Interrupter and the Advisor)

> When a narrative employs parenthesis, it lends depth. The reader is aware that there's more than one layer at work, whether it be as pleasing as a lover's whisper, or as disconcerting as a Shakespearian aside.
>
> — JOHN SMOLENS,
> critically acclaimed author of
> *Cold, The Invisible World,* and *Fire Point*

THE DASH is built to interrupt. It can strike with no warning, cut you off, stop conversations in its tracks, and redirect content any way it pleases. It is perhaps the most aggressive of all punctuation marks, and will grab the spotlight whether you like it or not. In fact, the word "dash" aptly derives from "to dash," or to shatter or strike violently.

When discussing the dash, most grammarians find it significant only inasmuch as it should not be confused with a hyphen; often it is relegated to a sign of carelessness. What a shame. The dash is a beautiful, striking mark of punctuation, which can enhance creativity, and which is crucial for capturing certain forms of dialogue. The dash can, of course, indicate haste and sloppiness (as we'll see below), but it must first be taken seriously before it can be dismissed.

Parentheses, on the other hand, respectfully interrupt you, so that you needn't cease speaking or change your train of thought. Their interruption is more of an enhancement, like a trusted advisor whispering in your ear. Like the dash, parentheses are often dismissed as a mere technical appliance. As with the dash, this is not where the discussion ends. Misused, of course, parentheses can be a terrible blight on a work, one that can make it nearly unreadable. But in the right hands, they can be a great creative tool, adding a layer of complexity to your text without interrupting its rhythm, one that could not exist any other way.

No creative writer is complete without knowing how to call upon and master these two marks.

HOW TO USE THEM

To truly grasp how to use dashes and parentheses, we must examine them together, comparing and contrasting their similarities and subtle differences. They are both interrupters; they both propel their subjects into the spotlight; are both used to digress, elucidate, or explain; and they perform a nearly identical function when the dash is used in pairs. To consider these marks separately (as many punctuation books do) is a mistake. Not only do they perform overlapping functions, but we learn more about each by holding them side by side.

- Dashes and parentheses are commonly used to indicate an aside or digression. Sometimes asides need to be interjected midsentence, whether to clarify or enhance. These asides could be removed and transformed into sentences of their own, but then you wouldn't achieve the same effect. Sometimes one needs to digress in the *midst* of a thought, in order to make the thought fuller or more complex. Such an aside takes a simple, straightforward thought and gives it a new dimension. Consider:

Buffaloes roamed freely in the Midwest in the 1800s.

This is a simple sentence. Using dashes or parentheses, though, we can enhance it, without requiring a new sentence. Consider:

Buffaloes roamed freely in the Midwest (some say in the Southwest, too) in the 1800s.

Buffaloes roamed freely in the Midwest in the 1800s—some say in the Southwest, too.

The asides add something; at the same time, while they pull us in another direction, they are also close enough to the main thought that they wouldn't work as sentences on their own. They are really sentence fragments, half ideas, looking for a place to land and needing the assistance of a dash or parentheses to give them a home.

In the above examples the parentheses and the dash, while serving the same purpose, went about it a different way. The parentheses allowed the aside to come in the middle of the sentence, while the dash demanded it be relegated to the end. This is implicit with the use of the solo dash, as it forces a clause to a sentence's end. Consequently, its effect is not exactly the same, since the aside following the dash feels more like an afterthought, and also prevents the sentence from carrying on. More importantly, it is not entirely appropriate. The aside in this case, for example, belongs in the middle of the sentence. The fact that buffaloes might have roamed "in the Southwest" is an aside to the fact that they roamed "in the Midwest" and thus needs to follow on the heels of that thought. By the end of the sentence we are already onto another thought (the 1800s), and thus we jar the reader by forcing him to go from the notions of geography to time and then back to geography again.

• There is a way, though, to allow the dash to function more like parentheses, and give it the flexibility to offset a clause midsentence. It's called the double dash.

Buffaloes roamed freely in the Midwest—some say in the Southwest, too—in the 1800s.

Yes, dashes can come in pairs. In fact, this is where dashes and parentheses share the most similar function: like parentheses, one dash opens a clause while the other dash closes it. As you can see from the above, the effect achieved is nearly identical to the effect achieved by parentheses; indeed, they are virtually interchangeable.

THE DIFFERENCE BETWEEN THE DOUBLE DASH AND PARENTHESES

I say "virtually" because there are some subtle differences between the double dash and parentheses. When you use a pair of dashes, it stops the flow of a sentence in its tracks, while parentheses allow a sentence to flow smoothly. For example:

Clocks made in Switzerland (particularly in Geneva) never break.

Clocks made in Switzerland—particularly in Geneva—never break.

It is the difference between a driver who politely interrupts you to point out a sight along the way and a driver who slams on the brakes.

Slam on the brakes (using dashes) when a point absolutely cannot be missed. Otherwise, like the jolted passenger, the reader will resent you, especially if you do it often, or without reason. It depends on your intention. If you want to subtly and smoothly offer a digression, if you want more streamlined prose, use parentheses. If you want to digress in a more forceful and dramatic way, use a pair of dashes.

There are some minor differences between them as well. A pair of parentheses can be used at the conclusion of a sentence, while a pair of dashes cannot. A pair of parentheses can enclose an independent sentence, while a pair of dashes cannot. And some might say that a parenthetical aside is a bit more formal, particularly those who believe dashes indicate casual writing. Consider:

Small windows let in less sunlight but (assuming it's winter) save you money on your heating bill.

Small windows let in less sunlight but—assuming it's winter— save you money on your heating bill.

In the above you might find the parentheses feel a bit more formal while the dashes a bit more casual, but this is a subtle distinction and can be argued either way.

Barring all of these differences, dashes and parentheses are interchangeable. You might want to alternate them for variety's sake, allowing you one more tool at your disposal.

• Regardless of their many specific functions, dashes and parentheses share one thing in common: they always propel a point into the limelight. These are not quiet punctuation marks, and it is nearly impossible for a clause to be offset by these marks and not shine in a sentence. Consider:

The Christmas tree business, and it is a business, is a multibillion-dollar one.

In this sentence, "and it is a business" doesn't really stand out as much as it could. But if we offset it with a pair of dashes:

The Christmas tree business—and it is a business—is a multi-billion-dollar one.

Now it is the very point of the sentence. The dash is especially powerful in this regard. In fact, if your intention is to make something stand out, dashes will be preferable to parentheses. Parentheses, in fact, tend to subdue an aside, to make it quieter; but nonetheless, the fact that it *is* an aside will always make it stand out to some degree.

Consider the opening sentence of E. M. Forster's novel *A Passage to India:*

Except for the Marabar Caves—and they are twenty miles off—the city of Chandrapore presents nothing extraordinary.

It is a bold decision to begin a book with a double dash. Few writers could pull it off without being overly stylistic, but Forster does, initiating one of the greatest novels of the twentieth century. In this case the dashes help to propel into the limelight the notion that these caves, the only thing extraordinary about Chandrapore, are "twenty miles off"; he's letting us know that not only is there nothing extraordinary about Chandrapore, but even the one thing that might be considered so is twenty miles away. He's hammering home the point that Chandrapore is a wasteland; indeed, after this sentence there follows a long description of the utter bleakness of the town.

Here's an example from David Leavitt's story "Gravity":

Theo had a choice between a drug that would save his sight and
a drug that would keep him alive, so he chose not to go blind. He
stopped the pills and started the injections—these required the
implantation of an unpleasant and painful catheter just above his
heart—and within a few days the clouds in his eyes started to clear
up, he could see again.

The dashes here convey shocking, painful material as an aside, in
an offhand way, allowing the sentence to carry on after such a dramatic clarification; by doing so, they show the insertion of a painful
catheter to be just one more in a long list of painful routines, help
demonstrate the tremendous amount of pain and discomfort
Theo's had to undergo with his treatments.

• Dashes and parentheses can be used to elucidate. The best writers
always reread their sentences and ask themselves how different
readers might interpret them. A sentence might, for example, be
too complex or ambiguous, or open to misinterpretation. Crafting
a sentence that can achieve a consensus of clarity is the mark of a
great writer (unless it is your intention to be ambiguous).
Sometimes the dash or parentheses can help achieve this clarity,
and can do so maximizing word economy and narrative flow. In
this example, a reader might be confused:

His friend came with us.

A reader might not know precisely which friend. But by adding a
short, clarifying clause (via parentheses), the intent can no longer
be mistaken:

His friend (the redhead) came with us.

The double dash can also fulfill this function, although not quite as smoothly:

His friend—the redhead—came with us.

Dashes and parentheses are particularly handy in clarifying a minor point in a pithy way. Few other punctuation marks offer this, can enable you to structure a sentence allowing for such a brief clarification. In the above example, for instance, you would not want to construct it as two sentences:

His friend came with us. She was a redhead.

The aside doesn't justify a sentence in its own right.

The function of clarification is primarily a technical one, but it needn't always be. Clarification can also be creative, can, for example, be a great tool for humor, irony, or sarcasm. It can help establish a running narrative by the viewpoint character, allow him commentary. For example:

He told me not to sit on the fire escape (as if I'd want to) because the structure was weak.

Mom seated me next to my (unbearable) cousin so we could talk all night.

Asides like these can also help distinguish viewpoint from description. If you decide to use them, they are better handled by parentheses than dashes.

Doris Lessing was fond of parentheses. She used them often in her story "To Room Nineteen":

That they had waited so long (but not too long) for this real thing
was to them a proof of their sensible discrimination. A good many
of their friends had married young, and now (they felt) probably
regretted lost opportunities; while others, still unmarried, seemed
to them arid, self-doubting, and likely to make desperate or
romantic marriages.

Here the parentheses are used to elucidate in a creative way, and
with just a few words powerfully capture the couple's viewpoint.
Notice how they allow the sentence to continue onward unimpeded, without stopping the narrative flow. They also allow more
information, and make for a richer thought.

• Dashes and parentheses can be used to indicate an afterthought.
This can help you take a simple thought and add a feeling of spontaneity:

I'd like you to come to dinner with me.

I'd like you to come to dinner with me — if you don't have other
plans.

Parentheses can also handle the task:

I'd like you to come to dinner with me (if you don't have other
plans).

Consider this example from Frank O'Connor's "Guests of the
Nation":

At dusk the big Englishman, Belcher, would shift his long legs out
of the ashes and say "Well, chums, what about it?" and Noble or
me would say "All right, chum" (for we had picked up some of

their curious expressions), and the little Englishman, Hawkins, would light the lamp and bring out the cards.

The parentheses here, used to indicate an afterthought, also serve to clarify, to explain why they're talking the way they are. Note also O'Connor's unusual usage of quotation marks here, his burying them in the midst of a longer sentence (we'll explore this in depth in a later chapter).

The dash, though, was born to indicate an afterthought, and in most cases is preferable for this purpose. In fact, the problem most people have with the dash is that it enables afterthoughts, which supposedly enables lazy writing, since good writing should be well thought out and not require afterthoughts. I agree this is the case when dealing with lazy or sloppy writing. But when it comes to writing crafted by a professional who toils over revision after revision, it is hard to sustain this argument. With such a writer, the writing is by its nature prefabricated, and if an afterthought is present, it is there deliberately. Sometimes it serves a creative purpose. For example, an afterthought can effectively capture the perspective of a scattered person, who constantly corrects himself:

I left my keys in the house—no, in the car.

• As we progress increasingly toward the creative, dashes and parentheses can help create a stream-of-consciousness style. The nature of these marks is to indicate asides, digressions, and afterthoughts, and this can be helpful when creating the illusion of writing unfolding in real time. Consider:

I went to the garden with the aim of uprooting that tree (the one near my window) but got distracted by the ringing phone and picked it up to realize—of all people—it was my grandmother who I hadn't talked to in years and who told me that she was relocating to Florida (where she was born) which was the last thing I wanted to hear.

In this extreme example we feel as if we're witnessing the narrator's thoughts unfolding as they hit the keys. Few marks facilitate this as well as dashes and parentheses. Creatively, there are times when such a style may be called for, for example, when capturing the voice of a character who thinks in such a way, or to mimic a diary entry.

> "There are only two books on earth that end with a double dash. First Laurence Sterne's *A Sentimental Journey*, published in 1766. Then, in honor of that mark, travel writer Jonathan Raban plays homage to Sterne by ending his book about sailing around England, *Coasting*, with a double dash."
>
> —PHYLLIS MOORE,
> author of *A Compendium of Skirts*

• Along these lines, dashes and parentheses can be used to help create a feeling of intimacy between you and the reader. These two marks create informality, create the illusion of your having dropped all pretense, and thus allow a reader to feel as if he's peeking into your private world. (Of course, the irony is that this sort of writing is even more calculated, to make it look spontaneous.) A work filled with dashes and parentheses will feel more intimate, perhaps even less intimidating. For example:

I ran into this guy—you know the type—who was all swagger and voice, filling the room with his obnoxious stories (they really were dreadful) and laughing at his own jokes until we'd all had enough.

Keep in mind, though, that intimacy is not one and the same with stream of consciousness; they often come hand in hand, but not necessarily so.

When establishing a narrative voice and style, you have to ask yourself whether you want to embrace the reader or keep him at arm's length. Both are effective; it depends on your intention. If the former, then dashes and parentheses can help you achieve your goal.

- Dashes and parentheses can help spice up one-dimensional writing. There may be places in your work where your writing is too dry, straightforward. It's inevitable to fall into this trap, given that a book can span several hundred pages. It could happen in a place where you're in a rush to convey facts, or where you hastily describe a setting or character you feel is insignificant. In such a case, dashes or parentheses can come to the rescue, not in and of themselves, but as mediums through which to add asides, tangents, and clarifications to lend the writing more depth and make it multidimensional. Consider:

He wanted to be a landscaper. My son, a landscaper. After four years of university and a hundred-thousand-dollar bill.

The writing here is not particularly complex. It's not witty or ironic, for example, and lacks a feeling of style and originality. But by incorporating a few dashes and parentheses, we open a gateway to another world:

He wanted to be a landscaper (of all things). My son—a Winston—a landscaper. After four years of university (and a good one at that) and a hundred-thousand-dollar bill.

This could be too stylistic for some reader's taste, too overdone, yet nonetheless, you see the difference in effect. Now there's a strong point of view, a running commentary. The writing feels more personal, more alive. Of course, what ultimately matters is the content between those dashes and parentheses, but none of it would be possible without those marks as a starting point.

There are some functions better suited for the dash than for parentheses. When it does not come in pairs, the dash is a loner, working on its own. It's also more casual than parentheses, less formal, and more flexible. Let's look specifically at some ways these two marks differ:

• A solo dash can be used to slam a sentence to a stop and change its direction. While parentheses can also effect a change of direction, their very nature (opening and closing parentheses) force them to return to the content at hand. The solo dash, though, has no such obligation. It can change a sentence without remorse, and keep on going. Consider:

I have to tell Dad that Mary called—did I leave my coat in the hallway?

The Civil War was fought with tens of thousands of soldiers—which reminds me, I need to schedule that trip to West Point.

The latter and former halves of the sentence are not connected, nor do they have to be. This is partly why the dash has gained such a bad reputation for "sloppiness." But such a technique could be used creatively, for example, to indicate the viewpoint of a character who is chaotic or scattered, who changes thoughts midsentence without returning to the original point.

• The solo dash can be used to indicate interruption, particularly in dialogue. Nothing can capture interruption in dialogue as well, and this alone makes its existence worthwhile. Many writers mistakenly indicate interruption with points of ellipsis, like this:

> "We can't tolerate your work here . . ."
> "If you're going to fire me, Fred, just get it over with."

This is incorrect. Ellipsis points indicate a trailing off, while a dash indicates a harsh break. This is an important distinction. It should really read like this:

> "We can't tolerate your work here—"
> "If you're going to fire me, Fred, just get it over with."

The beauty of this is that you can use it whenever you need to in dialogue—rarely will it feel overused.

The above was a basic example. For a more sophisticated usage, author Ellen Cooney offers a fine example of a use of the dash in literature, from Mary Shelley's *Frankenstein:*

> "What a place is this that you inhabit, my son!" said he, looking mournfully at the barred windows and wretched appearance of the room. "You travelled to seek happiness, but a fatality seems to pursue you. And poor Clerval—"
> The name of my unfortunate and murdered friend was an agitation too great to be endured in my weak state; I shed tears.

This example is unusual in that the dialogue is interrupted by action—the narrator's "shedding tears." The abrupt ending of dialogue, indicated by the dash, suggests that the person stops speaking as the result of the other's tears. Nothing more need be said: the dash does it all.

• The solo dash can also be used in dialogue to indicate hesitant, incoherent, or stumbling speech. For example:

> "If you don't mind, sir—excuse me for bothering you—you see I was just in the area—I thought you wouldn't—I had something to ask you and didn't know when—I hope this is a good time."

Parentheses, for their part, can perform some functions that the dash cannot:

• It is possible to enclose an entire, complete sentence with a pair of parentheses, something that cannot be done with a pair of dashes. Such a sentence could stand on its own, for instance in the midst of a paragraph, as a parenthetical aside to the sentence that preceded it. Of course, this parenthetical aside must be so complete that it merits its own sentence, a fairly unusual circumstance. As in:

> I'm on a strictly vegetarian diet. (Well, not strictly, I do eat fish from time to time.) The doctor says it will do wonders for my heart.

The aside is a complete thought, so it cannot fit in the midst of a sentence. Thus it is given its own sentence, made possible by parentheses.

Let's look at how dashes and parentheses were used by the masters. In *Notes from Underground*, Dostoyevsky used parentheses to establish a strong narrative style, and to break down the barrier between writer and reader:

> However, if irritated with all this idle talk (and I feel that you are irritated), you were to ask me who I really am, then I should reply, I'm a retired civil servant of humble rank, a collegiate assessor.

Dostoyevsky uses parentheses to interject personal asides, aimed directly at the reader, calling attention to the writing itself and to the writing process. Via a set of parentheses, he's created a feeling of intimacy, made the voice feel less formal, more spontaneous, and somehow more genuine. (Keep in mind, though, as we mentioned earlier, different translators can offer different versions of punctuation, so one cannot necessarily credit Dostoyevsky, who wrote in Russian, with the punctuation. Nonetheless, the intent of his prose shines through.)

John Edgar Wideman uses parentheses masterfully in his story "Fever":

> When they cut him open, the one who decided to stay, to be a beacon and steadfast, they will find: liver (1720 grams), spleen (150 grams), right kidney (190 grams), left kidney (180 grams), brain (1450 grams), heart (380 grams), and right next to his heart, the miniature hand of a child, frozen in a grasping gesture, fingers like hard tongues of flame, still reaching for the marvel of the beating heart, fascinated still, though the heart is cold, beats not, the hand as curious about this infinite stillness as it was about thump and heat and quickness.

What a powerful usage. On the surface, he seems to use parentheses to usher in mundane, technical information, but by using them this way, by reducing the vital organs to mere calculating weight measurements, he shows that they are anything but, and that we are dealing with a human being.

Joseph Conrad used the dash skillfully and abundantly. Take a close look at *Heart of Darkness* and you'll see that it is built on dashes. A superior example from that work:

> Two women, one fat and the other slim, sat on straw-bottomed chairs knitting black wool. The slim one got up and walked straight at me—still knitting with downcast eyes—and only just as I began to think of getting out of her way, as you would for a somnambulist, stood still, and looked up.

The strangeness of the image of these women knitting black wool in an empty building in the middle of a jungle—and additionally not stopping for anything—is brought to life by these two dashes. By using dashes to show the woman knitting as she walked, we can feel the narrator's surprise. The fact that she's still knitting actually belongs in its own sentence, but it is interjected into the middle of this sentence, just as the activity continues in the midst of her walking. The punctuation reflects the action. Indeed, this image reflects the entire book, one where people continue their civilized, futile actions in the midst of primitive surroundings.

> "One has to dismount from an idea, and get into the saddle again, at every parenthesis."
> —OLIVER WENDELL HOLMES

DANGER OF OVERUSE AND MISUSE

Dashes and parentheses are so conspicuous that any misuse will be spotted immediately. As with the colon, when these marks are absent, the reader won't mind; but when they are abundant, they can be intrusive in the extreme. The problems that come with these marks are diverse and many. Let's consider each in depth:

• Most obtrusive is the blatant overuse of these marks. Occasionally one will encounter the writer who is parenthetically obsessed, who uses the dash like a sword, slashing his way through every sentence. This alone can ruin a text. Consider:

> The emigration of Native Americans (as they are now called) was (to some extent) prodded by the arrival of the colonialists (the ones that survived), yet also a result of (according to those who witnessed it) a need for space.

Whenever you use parentheses you ask the reader to put a thought aside while you digress. It's like putting a caller on hold. Do it once, and they will tolerate it. Maybe even twice. But if you do it many times, they will likely get annoyed and hang up.

• Overly long clauses within dashes or parentheses are a common problem. When dashes or parentheses are used as a means to this end, the marks will detract too substantially from the main point, and risk the reader's not being able to get back on track. It's like putting someone on hold for ten minutes, then picking up, continuing midsentence, and expecting them to remember where you left off. For example:

> She showed up ten minutes late, wearing her black dress (the one she bought at Macy's with half her life's savings, the one we argued over endlessly and which she returned three times) and ringing my bell too long.

The main point is overwhelmed by the aside. An aside must be just that—an aside. It's hard enough to make a single point and keep it. If an aside must really be so substantial, then it needs its own sentence. Otherwise, you lose the intention of the sentence. Here, for example, the intention was to indicate that she "showed up late" and "rang the bell too long." But the sentence ended up being consumed by her dress.

• One of the easiest ways to grasp how to use the dash is to compare it to a punctuation mark with which it is commonly mistaken: the colon. The dash and colon share similar functions in that they both serve to offset a point. Yet there is a major difference between them. A colon signifies that the text that follows will be intrinsically related to the text that preceded it, for instance a culmination. A dash, though, can strike at any point in a sentence, and the text that follows needn't at all be related to what preceded it—indeed, a dash is more likely to herald a break in thought, an interruption, or aside. For example, you could write:

I'll take you with me—if you want to come.

But not:

I'll take you with me: if you want to come.

"If you want to come" is an afterthought, not a culmination, and as such a colon could not be used here.

Conversely, in most cases, a dash cannot be used where a colon is intended. For example, you could write:

Here's what I want to tell you: I love you.

But not:

Here's what I want to tell you—I love you.

"I love you" is the direct culmination of "Here's what I want to tell you," and as such a colon is necessary. Using a dash here would incorrectly denote an afterthought or aside.

That said, there is a function that the colon and dash share: setting the stage for an elaboration of the text that preceded them. Personally, I feel that this usage stretches the capacity of the dash, and that this function is best reserved for the colon. However, many master authors disagree, and have used it well for this purpose. Consider this example from Carol Bly's "The Tomcat's Wife":

We were making up the usual funeral spread—ground-up roast pork, ground-up roast beef, two onions chopped, three boiled egg yolks ground up, and Miracle Whip.

The dash works, sharing the colon's function. The dash also allows a less formal feeling, which could benefit a tallying up, such as above. Note Bly's masterful way of using a dash to offhandedly recite the "funeral spread," thus bringing the mundane to a profound event and making us realize they have experienced far too many funerals. F. Scott Fitzgerald uses the dash in this capacity, too, in *The Great Gatsby*:

About half way between West Egg and New York the motor-road hastily joins the railroad and runs beside it for a quarter of a mile so as to shrink away from a certain desolate area of land. This is a valley of ashes—a fantastic farm where ashes grow like wheat into ridges and hills and grotesque gardens, where ashes take the forms of houses and chimneys and rising smoke and finally, with a transcendent effort, of men who move dimly and already crumbling through the powdery air.

The dash here sets the stage for Fitzgerald to elaborate on what it means to be a "valley of ashes," the same function that could have been shared by the colon. Again, I prefer the use of the colon in this capacity, but you should at least know that the dash can be used this way.

• A common error is the use of only one dash when you intend to use two. Writers who haven't fully mastered the concept of the double dash sometimes begin an offset with a dash but never close it, leaving the reader to read on, wondering when the offset will end. Like this:

I took my kid to the ballgame—he'd been begging me for a year and we hit great weather.

A sentence like this will cause the reader to reread several times until he finally moves on in frustration. It's like a train that switches tracks, intending to return to the main track, but which never does. Ultimately, the reader will realize you made a mistake and that it's supposed to read like this:

I took my kid to the ballgame—he'd been begging me for a year— and we hit great weather.

Strangely enough, writers rarely make this mistake when using parentheses; perhaps the use of parentheses is so ingrained that they'd never consider beginning a parenthetical aside without closing it. But the double dash is not always given the same respect.

- Finally, some sentences use parentheses as a crutch. As Charles Boyd said in his 1928 *Grammar for Great and Small*, "The test of a parenthesis is whether the other words make sense without it." How true. Parentheses should embellish the sentence at hand — but never be integral for its construction. For example, if we take this sentence:

> The building was constructed (the old-fashioned way) and thus could withstand any storm.

and remove the parenthetical aside, we see that the sentence does not work without it:

> The building was constructed and thus could withstand any storm.

Thus we see that it was not truly a parenthetical aside, and parentheses must not be used:

> The building was constructed the old-fashioned way and thus could withstand any storm.

If a sentence can't work on its own after you remove the parentheses, then the parentheses aren't being used properly. They should be removed, and the sentence reconstructed.

CONTEXT

When everything is an aside, nothing is. Overused dashes and parentheses detract from each other's power. The writer who rarely uses these marks will be able to use one for maximum effect when he needs to. Be sparing, and always consider the context of the greater work.

- Dashes and parentheses are attention grabbing, and will dominate a sentence and squeeze other punctuation marks out of the way. For example, the dash as afterthought will detract from the power of the period: if a sentence is brought to a near halt just before its end, the period will pack little punch. When debating whether to employ a dash or parentheses, consider whether you can afford to lessen the power of a nearby comma, semicolon, or period. Which mark needs to have the greatest impact in order to capture the intent of the sentence? Consider this example from Daniel Meyerson's *The Linguist and the Emperor*:

> Thus proclaims the "midwife"—Robespierre the "Incorruptible"—a skillful orator whose stirring speeches have helped him seize power (a power maintained with denunciations and spies and fanatic scoundrels).

Here Meyerson uses both a pair of dashes and parentheses in a single sentence, allowing for a much richer, more interesting, and more complex sentence. Notice, though, how strong the usage of dashes and parentheses is, and how it will make other punctuation marks pale by comparison.

- Keep in mind that dashes and parentheses aren't the only marks that can offset: a pair of commas can handle this task, too. A comma offset isn't as striking or powerful as an offset with a pair of dashes or parentheses, and it's not as versatile either, since when using commas, the material in the offset must be intrinsically related to the rest of the sentence. Nonetheless, commas can perform this task. For example:

> I told Jennifer that I missed her and that—if she wanted—I'd write to her.

Can also be:

> I told Jennifer that I missed her and that, if she wanted, I'd write
> to her.

There may be some instances when you'll want to replace your
dashes or parentheses with a pair of commas, since a pair of commas allows the smoothest sentence flow and is less jarring than
dashes or even parentheses. Alternately, you may want to replace a
comma offset with dashes and parentheses if you want more of an
impact, or if you already have too many commas in a sentence.
Indeed, dashes or parentheses can be effective in helping prevent
confusion in a comma-laden sentence.

• Likewise, dashes and parentheses aren't the only marks that can
indicate an afterthought. Commas can perform this function, too:

> I was going to tell those kids to stop screaming—but I fell back
> asleep.

Can also be:

> I was going to tell those kids to stop screaming, but I fell back
> asleep.

A period can handle this task, too:

> I was going to tell those kids to stop screaming. But I fell back
> asleep.

As you see, using a comma to create an afterthought doesn't quite
give it the same punch, while using a period lends it a discon-

nected feeling. And neither of these is quite as effective or natural as the dash. It depends on your intended effect. Realize there are options before rushing to use the dash or parentheses as your tool of choice. Let's conclude with an example from Melville, who relied on dashes often. Here's an excerpt from his story, "The Paradise of Bachelors and the Tartarus of Maids":

> Sick with the din and soiled with the mud of Fleet Street—where the Benedick tradesmen are hurrying by, with ledger-lines rules along their brows, thinking upon rise of bread and fall of babies— you adroitly turn a mystic corner—not a street—glide down a dim, monastic, way, flanked by dark, sedate, and solemn piles, and still wending on, give the whole care-worn world the slip, and, disentangled, stand beneath the quiet cloisters of the Paradise of Bachelors.

Here Melville manages to use four dashes in a single sentence, helping to prolong it. Such a long sentence gives us the feeling of descending deeper into the setting, of turning corners, walking down streets. Note also the abundant commas here, making us pause at each turn, also forcing us to slow, to take it all in. The punctuation here truly reflects the content, and helps bring it to life.

WHAT YOUR USE OF DASHES AND PARENTHESES REVEALS ABOUT YOU

The Dash

A text filled with dashes could be indicative of different problems, depending upon whether the writer is advanced or amateur. With the advanced writer, the overuse of the dash (particularly the solo dash) indicates a writer who is overly stylistic. This writer strives to create a feeling of informality, of intimacy between himself and the reader, and his chief objective is to prove his lack of calculation. Yet the fact that he goes to such ends indicates an even greater degree of calculation. He is too concerned with the impression he'll make, too eager for the reader's approval. Of course, by seeking it, he will lose it.

With the amateur writer, the overuse of the dash indicates simple laziness and sloppiness. It is the writer who puts no stake on revision, who accepts his first draft as is. It also belies scattered thought.

The writer who underuses the dash is too concerned with formality, too unwilling to experiment. He won't put himself on the line enough, and his characters might also stop short of an ultimate journey, discovery, or revelation. This writer is safe. The good news, though, is that he is less inclined to be a scattered thinker, and more likely to put greater emphasis on revision.

Parentheses

One might overuse parentheses for a variety of reasons. In the amateur or sloppy writer, the overuse of these marks generally indicates scattered thinking. It also indicates an aversion to revise (perhaps for egotistical reasons, perhaps out of laziness), or a willingness to revise but an inability to catch one's own errors upon revision. Not every writer is a good editor for his own work.

The overuse of these marks could also be driven by an academic impulse to not omit any detail. Such writers think that merely moving a footnote into the main text (via a parenthetical aside) somehow makes it okay. It does not. In mainstream books, footnotes should stay where they are—at the bottom of the page, after the chapter, or in the back of the book—or better yet, be deleted altogether. You should find a way to say what needs to be said in the text itself. Facts are for encyclopedias. An unimpeded reading experience is for books.

The overuse of these marks can be driven by an impulse to avoid taking a firm stance. There is no greater way to sneak in a qualification than with a dash or parentheses. Readers, though, yearn for confident, authoritative prose, and a text filled with qualifications will only make them respect you less.

These marks might be overused as a way of escaping developing your main thought or argument. When one indulges in asides, it becomes easy to avoid a single point. This might arise from a lack of confidence in your own authority. One might also overuse these marks because one is an overzealous stylist, too desperate to create a feeling of intimacy or spontaneity. Ironically, such a style is even more calculating, since writing is crafted. Readers will often see through it and simply be turned off.

In general, the writer who overuses parentheses (or the double dash) is likely to think in digression. He will have a short attention span, be easily distracted, and be overflowing with knowledge, impatient to get it all in. He will likely write a longer, more uncensored book. Not as concerned with the reader as he should be, he puts too much stake in his own powers and in his first draft, unwilling to go back and rewrite so that parentheses are not needed in the first place. This writer is more likely to be spontaneous. He is more likely to lose his train of thought, to begin a paragraph on one note and end it on another. He will probably write a richer, less expected text, but will also be harder to follow—often not in a good way.

Since the use of parentheses often indicates a writer who is spontaneous, spur of the moment, who allows room for digressions and asides, the writer who underuses parentheses is more likely to be less spontaneous, to be more calculating, more formal. The good news is that he knows that information should go in its proper place, and will be a straight thinker. This, though, is a double-edged sword, as this writer is more likely to leave digressionary material out, possibly at the expense of crafting a less rich work. He might be too focused on the narrow road ahead, and less willing to explore detours on the course of the journey.

EXERCISES

• Tally up your number of dashes and parentheses in one of your works. How many of each appear on the first page? In the first chapter? If you find more than two parenthetical or double dash asides per page, it is likely too much. Conversely, if you find you don't use them at all, your writing may be too calculated, not as rich as it should be. The first step is awareness.

• In many cases, parenthetical or double dash asides are either best converted to sentences in their own right, or not used at all. Examine each and ask yourself if it is truly necessary. Can any be deleted? If not, ask yourself if the digressionary material must remain in the midst of a sentence. Can it be given its own sentence?

• Do any parenthetical or double dash asides in your work contain too-long clauses? Look for any long asides and ask yourself if the main thought is compromised or weakened as a result. Can any be shortened? Cut? Given their own sentences?

• As mentioned previously, dashes and parentheses can be used to spice up sections of writing that feel too simplistic or straightforward. Are there any such areas in your work? Using a pair of dashes or parentheses, add an aside or two. Be less constrained. How does it transform the writing?

QUOTATION MARKS

(the Trumpets)

The quotation mark distinguishes between what's thought and said, between the interior and exterior of a character's mind. And since Joyce blurred that distinction in A *Portrait of the Artist as a Young Man*, it can be used to help orient the reader, but should never be used to intrude or dumb down the narrative. Hemingway and Carver use quotation marks to brilliant effect; their dialogue crackles and snaps, but their quotation marks never slow the reader down, nor make the dialogue feel written. One always feels with them that you're in the room, listening to real people talk, and you cease to see the quotation marks. That finally is the great use of this piece of punctuation—that you don't notice it's there.

—PAUL CODY,

critically acclaimed author of *Shooting the Heart*

QUOTATION MARKS are the most visible marks in the world of punctuation. They are raised above the text, dangling conspicuously; they come in pairs, offering twice the impact; and their presence often demands the indentation of a paragraph, allowing them to be roomily indented from the margin. As if all this were not dramatic and eye catching enough, they also often work in a pack, with one pair of quotation marks following another, cascading down the page, each demanding a new paragraph and new indentation. They add visibility to visibility until they dominate the page.

Quotation marks are also unique in that they indicate the end of one world (prose) and the beginning of another (dialogue), and as such are one of the most powerful tools with which to propel context into the limelight. Indeed, to discuss quotation marks—their presence, absence, overuse, underuse—is to discuss dialogue itself. And their usage, of course, is not just limited to dialogue: they can offset individual words or phrases to indicate irony, sarcasm, or a special meaning. Indeed, it is impossible to hear these siren calls and *not* pay attention. As such, they are the trumpets of the punctuation world.

HOW TO USE THEM

Quotation marks are more flexible than most writers assume. Often they are used in a merely functional way, which is a pity, because they can subtly enhance your writing. Some of the ways they can be used:

• To alter the pace. Dialogue is the great accelerator. Nothing has its power on pace, whether to speed a text or slow it down. Open any book and you'll find the reading experience accelerates greatly when you reach a stretch of dialogue; read a screenplay and you'll find yourself turning pages two or three times faster than with a book. Traditional dialogue cannot be indicated without quotation marks (in English, at least—quotation marks are not the norm for dialogue in Spanish, French, Italian, or Russian literature) and in this sense, the two are codependent.

Thus, creatively, the presence of quotation marks accelerates the pace of your work. This can be useful in places where the pace slows, for example, where there are long stretches of prose. Alternately, removing quotation marks will slow the pace significantly. This can be useful in places where the pace is too fast, where a reader needs grounding and time to process.

Consider this example from Tobias Wolff's story "Mortals":

"So what happened?" the metro editor said to me.

"I wish I knew."

"That's not good enough," the woman said.

"Dolly's pretty upset," Givens said.

"She has every right to be upset," the metro editor said. "Who called in the notice?" he asked me.

"To tell the truth, I don't remember. I suppose it was somebody from the funeral home."

"You call them back?"

"I don't believe I did, no."

"Check with the family?"

"He most certainly did not," Mrs. Givens said.

"No," I said.

Notice how the abundant quotation marks accelerate the pace, keep it moving at a fast clip (of course, this effect is compounded greatly by the short lines of speech). It feels as if the dialogue fires back and forth, with little pause in between. The result is a much faster reading experience. Of course, one would not want to maintain this for an entire book, but after a long stretch of prose, a stretch of dialogue like this allows the reader a rest stop. In Wolff's case, it also evokes a clipped, matter-of-fact tone, which brilliantly captures the newsroom atmosphere.

• Quotation marks can allow a break from prose. Every book really offers two worlds: the world of prose and the world of dialogue. They do a dance, speeding up the work, slowing it down, setting the stage for a scene, letting it play out. Readers are subconsciously aware of this, and will sometimes scan the prose until they find a stretch of dialogue; when really impatient, as when caught up in a thriller, they might even first scan down to the dialogue to see what happens, then back up to the prose. It's as if prose and dialogue are two different entities living in the same book.

Dialogue allows the reader a visual break from prose, from sentences that can stretch across the entire page. Reaching a stretch of dialogue is like stretching one's legs after a long car ride: it gives readers the renewed vigor they need to get back onto the road, into the thick world of prose. Such a break would not be possible without quotation marks and their requisite spacing.

• Quotation marks can help indicate a passage of time. Most writers just routinely use quotation marks to open and close a line of dialogue; they rarely consider the placement of the marks *within* a line of dialogue. For example:

"I love you, don't you know that?" he said.

This is the standard usage, as it should be. But quotation marks needn't always be so straightforward. They can be rearranged within dialogue to create subtle effects. One such effect is to create the feeling of a passage of time. Watch what happens when we break up the quotation marks:

"I love you," he said, "don't you know that?"

Now there exists a slight pause between "I love you" and "don't you know that?" that might better suit the scene, depending on the writer's intention. This can be taken even further:

"I love you," he said. "Don't you know that?"

Here a period follows "he said" and "Don't you know that?" is begun with a capital, indicating a new sentence. This suggests even more finality after "I love you," and an even longer passage of time. Through the rearrangement of quotation marks, we have created a whole new feeling for the same line of dialogue. Of course, the quotation marks couldn't achieve what they do here without some help from the comma and the period. We are beginning to see how interdependent punctuation marks are (we'll explore this later).

Here's an example from John Smolens's novel *Cold*:

"All right," she said. "You can come inside."

He began walking immediately, his legs lifting up out of the deep snow.

"Slowly," she said. "And put your hands down at your sides where I can see them."

By breaking up the dialogue with additional sets of quotation marks, Smolens makes us feel the pause within the speech, makes us feel time slowing down as she sums him up and decides what to do.

• Quotation marks can help create a feeling of revelation or finality to dialogue. For example:

He said, "I love you, don't you know that?"

Prefacing the dialogue with "he said" is a usage rarely employed, as it should be. It is not for everyday use, as it draws much attention. Still, there are times when you might want to have the option. Placing the quotation marks in this way suggests that the dialogue to follow will be more measured, more final, possibly even a revelation. The effect is subtle. If we insert a colon, its effect becomes more apparent:

He said: "I love you, don't you know that?"

Notice the feeling of finality that comes with this; it feels as if this line of dialogue will conclude a scene—indeed, it would be hard to continue dialogue in the wake of this.

Stephen Crane goes so far as to conclude his story "The Little Regiment" with a set of quotation marks:

> After a series of shiftings, it occurred naturally that the man with the bandage was very near to the man who saw the flames. He paused, and there was a little silence. Finally he said: "Hello, Dan." "Hello, Billie."

The colon preceding the first line of dialogue really makes us feel the pause, while the paragraph break before the final line makes us feel it even further. In context, the fact that these quotations come at the end of a paragraph makes us feel their weight even more. It is a powerful way to end a story.

• Quotation marks can help break up long stretches of dialogue. Just as long stretches of prose can be tiresome, so can long exchanges of dialogue. The pace can become too fast, causing the work to feel ungrounded. If you have a character who is long winded, for example, or prone to making speeches, his rants can grow weary on a reader. Consider:

> "I can't see anything at night since my operation. The doctor said the glare would go away, but it hasn't. Big surprise. I've never met any doctor who told me the truth. Doctors are all alike. I swear,

I'd be happy never seeing one again. Care for a brandy?"

This is a lot for a reader to take in at once; more importantly, it is disconcerting, as the speaker changes topics without pausing. But by manipulating the quotation marks, we can provide a natural rest and give the reader the energy he needs to go on:

"I can't see anything at night since my operation. The doctor said the glare would go away, but it hasn't. Big surprise. I've never met any doctor who told me the truth. Doctors are all alike. I swear, I'd be happy never seeing one again," he said. "Care for a brandy?"

If you opt to break up the dialogue this way, the break must come at an instant when the speaker might naturally pause in his speech, for example, at a moment when he'd like something to sink in. In real life, few people speak in uninterrupted speeches; natural pauses abound in dialogue, when speakers shift in their chairs, cross their legs, sip coffee, or look out a window. It is your task to find them.

Breaking up dialogue with quotation marks serves another purpose: it can help clarify who's speaking, which might be necessary in a long back-and-forth between multiple characters. Consider:

Jack and Dave entered the room.
"Do you have any scotch? I could use a drink."
"I don't think so. Check in the cupboard."

You never want readers to waste their precious energy on trying to figure out who is speaking. Inserting a few extra quotation marks, though, can make all the difference:

Jack and Dave entered the room.
"Do you have any scotch?" Jack asked. "I could use a drink."
"I don't think so. Check in the cupboard."

Alternately:

Jack and Dave entered the room.
"Do you have any scotch? I could use a drink."
"I don't think so," Dave answered. "Check in the cupboard."

Notice how you only have to break up dialogue once, and it clarifies everyone who is speaking. Either of these are acceptable, although it's preferable to identify who is speaking immediately so that the reader doesn't have to waste any energy deciphering.

• Sometimes quotation marks can have the greatest impact by not appearing at all. When dialogue is called for, quotation marks are expected; but if they are absent, it has a strong effect. To convey dialogue without traditional quotation marks, you need to either use some other mark, like a dash (which I don't recommend and which we'll explore in depth below), or paraphrase. For example:

She said she didn't want to talk to me anymore.

There are times when paraphrasing can be quite effective. For one, paraphrased dialogue is filtered through another character's viewpoint or recollection, which means it becomes equally about the character conveying it. For instance, in the above example, did she really say she didn't want to talk to the narrator, or was that his perception of it, or was he outright lying? It's like the game of telephone: by the time it gets to you, it is often changed in at least some way. Who changed it—and how—is often more interesting than the dialogue itself.

• Finally, quotation marks needn't only be used for dialogue. They have a creative usage outside the realm of dialogue, which is to couch individual words or phrases to indicate they are not meant to be read literally. They can alter the way you read a word or phrase in many ways, for example, to indicate irony or sarcasm. As Lynne Truss says in *Eats, Shoots & Leaves*, quotation marks "are sometimes used by fastidious writers as a kind of linguistic rubber glove, distancing them from vulgar words or clichés they are too refined to use in the normal way." For example:

Yeah, it was really "cold." I had to shed two shirts just to stop sweating. It's the last time I listen to her.

The banker's "smile" sent shivers through my spine.

Quotation marks around individual words might also indicate that we are reading someone's interpretation of a word or phrase:

My piano teacher gave me another "lesson." It wasn't a lesson at all. We played for two minutes, and he spent the rest of the hour trying to pick me up. What a jerk.

Let's look at some examples from literature. Dan Chaon uses this technique well in his short story "Big Me":

Before that, everything was a peaceful blur of childhood, growing up in the small town of Beck, Nebraska. A "town," we called it. Really, the population was just less than two hundred, and it was one of those dots along Highway 30 that people didn't usually

even slow down for, though strangers sometimes stopped at the little gas station near the grain elevator, or ate at the café.

By putting it in quotation marks, the word "town" here is not meant to
be taken literally; indeed, Chaon goes on to explain exactly what that
"town" consisted of. Elizabeth Barrett Browning uses a similar technique in her "Sonnet 20" from her *Sonnets from the Portuguese:*

> Say over again, and yet once over again,
> That thou dost love me. Though the word repeated
> Should seem "a cuckoo-song," as thou dost treat it,
> Remember, never to the hill or plain,
> Valley and wood, without her cuckoo-strain
> Comes the fresh Spring in all her green completed.

Here she quotes her lover, and then plays on the meaning of that
quote, transforming it into an analogy of spring, and of something
transcendent.
In any of these ways, quotation marks can transform a word or phrase
into something which it is not.

"Speech has a prodigious non-verbal arsenal: pitch,
stress, pause, intonation, facial expression, gesture,
body language. It was to make up for the loss of
speech accoutrements that punctuation gradually
developed."
—RENE J. CAPPON,
The Associated Press Guide to Punctuation

Let's look at some more examples from classic literature. Flannery O'Connor used quotation marks brilliantly. Here's an excerpt from her short story "Revelation":

> Mrs. Turpin put a firm hand on Claud's shoulder and said in a voice that included anyone who wanted to listen, "Claud, you sit in that chair there," and gave him a push down into the vacant one.

Instead of following convention and putting the quotation in its own paragraph, O'Connor, in the midst of one long sentence, winds up into the quotation and winds down afterward, burying the quotation inside. By doing this, the quotation feels like an extension of the action, subtly makes us feels as if there is no distinction between Mrs. Turpin's acting and speaking; especially since she doesn't wait for a response, it feels as if her dialogue is a command—not a question. This is perfectly in line with her character and her relationship to Claud, as she is indeed bossy and overwhelming, and does everything at once, in a rush. All of this is captured by the well-placed quotation marks.

Kafka was equally adept with quotation marks. Consider the opening line of his famous story "In the Penal Colony":

> "It's a remarkable piece of apparatus," said the officer to the explorer and surveyed with a certain air of admiration the apparatus which was after all quite familiar to him.

Kafka could have also followed convention and placed a period just before the concluding quotation marks, or after "officer," or after "explorer." But he chose not to do any of these things, to rather extend the sentence well past where it would normally end. All of this reflects on the quotation marks, since they initiate the sentence. Here, the extended sentence perfectly captures the mindset of the officer, a man who is so anxious to show off his apparatus that he can barely finish speaking before he is already surveying it. Indeed, Kafka captures the very crux of the story in a single sentence. (Again, keep in mind that punctuation in translation is open to interpretation.)

John Updike uses quotation marks skillfully in his story "A&P":

> The girls, and who would blame them, are in a hurry to get out, so I say "I quit" to Lengel quick enough for them to hear, hoping they'll stop and watch me, their unsuspected hero.

The fact that the narrator quits is actually a significant moment in the story; yet it is buried here, hidden in quotation marks in the midst of a longer sentence. Updike wants to make readers work here, to make sure they are reading closely. He also, with the placement of these quotation marks, reflects the content, evoking the feeling of a boy quitting in midsentence, in midaction, spontaneously and unsure of himself.

> . . . It was also ridiculous, unjust, and because he had always been a religious man, it was in a way an affront to God. Manischevitz believed this in all his suffering. When his burden had grown too crushingly heavy to be borne he prayed in his chair with shut hollow eyes: "My dear God, sweetheart, did I deserve that this should happen to me?" Then recognizing the worthlessness of it, he put aside the complaint and prayed humbly for assistance: "Give Fanny back her health, and to me for myself that I shouldn't feel pain in every step. Help now or tomorrow is too late. This I don't have to tell you." And Manischevitz wept.

This comes from Bernard Malamud's "Angel Levine." It is a remarkable use of quotation marks. Instead of giving each quotation its own paragraph and indentation (as one normally would), Malamud buries them toward the end of a long paragraph (the paragraph was much longer than this, redacted for this example). And then to cap it off, he does not conclude the paragraph with a quotation, but continues with one last sentence, burying the quotations even further. The feeling evoked is one of despair, of drowning, of dialogue that goes unanswered and of a man at the end of his rope.

DANGER OF OVERUSE AND MISUSE

An abundance of quotation marks means an abundance of dialogue. A text dominated by dialogue will usually have an uneven, too-fast pace; it will often not be grounded in character, plot, or setting, the fundamentals of a book. This holds equally true for a work absent of quotation marks (and thus dialogue). Such a work will be dominated by prose, and it won't take long before the reader feels like he is struggling for air. The pace will slow to a crawl, and the chances of a reader staying with it will grow less likely with every page. Excessive dialogue can work in a screenplay, but a novel is a different medium, one which requires a dance between dialogue and prose, that each be given proper space and time. If a book leans too much in either direction, it can feel lopsided.

You must find the right balance between these two worlds, not always easy to do. There will be moments in your work that can use speeding up, and moments that will benefit by slowing down. Outside readers can help you get an objective eye on this, but in the meantime, if you are unsure, look to the quotation marks and you will be given an immediate picture. Many ailments can show themselves to you:

• Some writers rearrange the order of quotation marks within dialogue for no real reason. Few things are more jarring than having the position of quotation marks alternate with every line of dialogue. For example:

She said, "Pass the sugar."
"It's over there," I said, "beside the ketchup."
"Don't get snide with me," she answered.
I said, "I'm not."

The alternating distracts from the dialogue itself, and worse, does so for no real reason. It is a mistake some amateur writers make. Quotation marks must never be moved within dialogue unless there is an important reason for doing so.

• In some trendy works (and classic works, too) you'll find that authors opt not to use quotation marks at all, but rather to indicate dialogue with some other mark, such as a dash, or italics, or no mark at all (not to be confused with paraphrasing). For example:

   —I don't want your computer. I told you, I don't have any place to put it.
   —But it's not that old.
   —That's what you said last time. And you stuck me with a 1942 dishwasher.

They won't use the quotation mark to differentiate dialogue, but will rather let dialogue blend with the rest of the text. Even some great authors have done this, notably James Joyce or, more recently, Cormac McCarthy. Presumably this is done for the sake of being different, but to my mind this is just stylistic, and it makes it unnecessarily hard on the reader. Why boycott quotation marks? The quotation mark does its job very well: it's unique and highly visible. It is as near perfect as a punctuation mark could hope to be. It was invented in the first place because there was a need for a mark to help clearly indicate dialogue. Omitting it, or refusing to indent, or replacing it with dashes, will just confuse a reader.

There are, of course, exceptions. As I mentioned, even great authors have crafted works that, for whatever reason, avoided quotation marks. Consider this example from William Carlos Williams's "The Use of Force":

They were new patients to me, all I had was the name, Olson. Please come down as soon as you can, my daughter is very sick. When I arrived I was met by the mother, a big startled looking woman, very clean and apologetic who merely said, Is this the doctor? and let me in. In the back, she added. You must excuse us, doctor, we have her in the kitchen where it is warm. It is very damp here sometimes.

Williams is a brilliant writer, and this is an exceptional short story, and I can understand why he avoided quotation marks. That said, I nonetheless would have preferred to have them here; I feel it just burdens the reader with unnecessary effort, and diverts the energy to trying to decipher who is speaking.

• Occasionally one encounters a work where quotation marks are used heavily to offset individual words, often in order to indicate irony or sarcasm. For example:

He said I didn't have an "eye" for detail, that I didn't "know" what to do, that I was just "beginning" to enter this world—like he's such an "expert."

Such works usually come hand in hand with flippant writing, where a cynical tone prevails. The problem with this, aside from being stylistic, is that it becomes a safety cushion. When every other word is encapsulated by quotation marks to indicate irony or sarcasm, the writer clearly uses it as an escape, to avoid definitively taking a stand himself. Eventually it will lose its effect and turn readers off.

CONTEXT

Quotation marks are the quintessential team player. They never muscle other punctuation marks out of their way—on the contrary, they need and embrace them. As we saw above, quotation marks by themselves can only go so far in creating an effect. If they want to indicate pauses, breaks, and momentous moments in dialogue, they need help from the comma, period, dash, and colon. Let's look at some of the ways they work together:

• Without the comma, quotation marks cannot even conclude a basic line of dialogue:

"I'm going to the laundry," he said.

They also need commas to indicate a pause, and to continue dialogue:

"I'm going to the laundry," he said, "and you're not coming with me."

• Periods are equally needed by quotation marks, since dialogue cannot be concluded without them:

"I'm going to the laundry."

• Quotation marks need colons if they want to help indicate finality or a revelation:

I looked at him and said: "Don't ever talk to me again."

• And without dashes, quotation marks couldn't indicate interruption:

"I really don't think you should—"
"I don't care what you think," he said.

Just about the only marks that don't do well with quotation marks are semicolons and parentheses. Theoretically these marks can be used within dialogue, but they are hard to hear within speech and are thus better suited for prose.

• Dialogue itself is all about context. Too much prose without dialogue is anathema, while too much dialogue without prose is equally so. One must develop an ear for knowing when prose needs a break, and when dialogue needs to curtail itself. It's a delicate balance, and quotation marks are the great indicator. Consider this fine example from Katherine Anne Porter's story "The Martyr":

When earnest-minded people made pilgrimages down the narrow, cobbled street, picked their way carefully over puddles in the patio, and clattered up the uncertain stairs for a glimpse of the great and yet so simple personage, she would cry, "Here come the pretty sheep!" She enjoyed their gaze of wonder at her daring.

Here the dialogue stands out, as it comes on the heels of such a long sentence, such a long stretch of prose. It almost feels as if the long sentence is building momentum, which culminates with the quotation.

> "Although the authorized version of the Bible is abuzz with speeches, dialogue and discussion, there is not a single quotation mark in sight. This would hardly do today.
>
> —GRAHAM KING, *Collins Good Punctuation*

WHAT YOUR USE OF QUOTATION MARKS REVEALS ABOUT YOU

In many cases, a publishing professional need only flip through a manuscript to get an immediate idea of its worth: quotation marks tell the story.

A writer who overuses dialogue (and thus quotation marks) doesn't have an acute sense of pacing, doesn't realize that a work can progress too fast. He relies heavily on dialogue, which means he's also using it poorly, since overuse comes hand in hand with misuse. He might, for instance, be using dialogue as a means of conveying information. He is more likely a beginner, plot oriented, and anxious for a fast pace. Alternately, he might be a playwright or screenwriter-turned-author, stuck in the remnants of his previous form. In either case, he is more likely to neglect setting and character development. He is impatient, believes too much in the power of speech, and not enough in the power of silence. And since dialogue rates fairly high on the drama scale, this writer is likely to be overdramatic.

The good news is that he strives for drama, and aims to please the reader. Additionally, his abundance of dialogue means an abundance of character interaction, which means he at least strives to bring his characters together and create scenes between them.

The writer who overuses quotation marks for another purpose—to offset individual words or phrases—is more likely insecure. He couches a plethora of words behind the security of quotation marks, either to quote someone else or to indicate irony or sarcasm, and thus is afraid to simply state things in his own right. He is more likely to be cynical, and needs to realize that at some point readers will want seriousness and confidence. The good news for him, though, is that he will likely take himself less seriously and be at least somewhat funny, both positive traits that offer much promise.

The writer who underuses quotation marks (resulting in too little dialogue) is rare. He is more likely to be a serious literary author and have great faith in the power of prose. He is more likely to be a silent type, to be internal. All of this bodes well. Unfortunately, though, he is also likely to be self-indulgent, to think of pleasing himself rather than readers. His work will be slow going, often deadly so, since he doesn't grasp that most readers need to move at a quick pace. He is likely to rely too heavily on description, and since dialogue brings scenes and drama, its absence means that he might not think enough in terms of heightened moments. There will be issues with his characters, too: either individually the characters won't be interesting enough to have much to say, or collectively he's created a population that just doesn't interact very well. If there is a pool of characters in a work with a lot to say to one another, dialogue will come whether you like it or not. Such a forum cannot exist in a work devoid of quotation marks.

EXERCISES

- Look over the dialogue in one of your works and choose a moment where a character pauses yet where it's not indicated. Break up the quotation at the appropriate moment by encapsulating one pair of quotation marks with a "he said" and then adding a new pair to continue the dialogue. What impact does it have? Can you apply this technique elsewhere in your work?

- Choose a stretch of dialogue that feels like it goes on too long. Use the above technique to break up the quotation marks at a moment where the reader might grow weary. What impact does it have? Can you apply this technique elsewhere in your work?

- Choose an exchange of dialogue that involves multiple characters, one where it might be hard to keep track of who's speaking. Use the above technique to break up the quotation marks at a place where the reader might be confused, following the quotation with "NAME [fill in the name of your character] said." Does this add clarity? Can you apply this technique elsewhere in your work?

- Choose an area of your work that has a disproportionate amount of dialogue. Delete some of the dialogue. Paraphrase it instead, having one character convey to another what someone else said. What difference does this make? Can you apply this technique elsewhere in your work?

- If your work underuses quotation marks (and thus dialogue), rethink your character choices. Either adjust your current characters or go back to the drawing board and create new characters that—collectively—have a lot to say each other, a lot to get off their minds. Put them in a scene together. What impact does it have?

THE PARAGRAPH AND SECTION BREAKS

(the Stoplight and the Town Line)

Look to the paragraphs, and the discourse will take care of itself.

—old maxim

FEW PEOPLE would think of the paragraph break as a punctuation mark, but it certainly is. In ancient times there were no paragraphs—sentences simply flowed into one another without interruption—but over time text became segmented into paragraphs, first indicated by the capital letter "C." During medieval times this mark evolved into the paragraph symbol [¶] (called a pilcrow or a paraph) and this eventually evolved into the modern-day paragraph break, which is, of course, indicated today by only a line break and indentation. The indentation we use today was originally there for early printers, so that they would have space for the large illuminated letter that used to herald paragraphs. The illuminated letter no longer exists, but, luckily for tired readers, the spacing does.

Today the paragraph break is indicated only by absence, which is perhaps why it is glossed over in discussions about punctuation. This is a shame, because it is one of the most crucial marks in the punctuation world. It is used thousands of times in any given book, and it alone can make or break a work. Few places are more visible than the beginnings and endings of paragraphs: with their ample spacing, they are eye catching. As such the paragraph break has an unparalleled ability to propel into the limelight, offering perpetual opportunities to grab readers with new hooks. It has the unique power to frame a cluster of sentences, to give them shape and meaning, to resolve the theme of the current paragraph and set the stage for the paragraph to come. Indeed, this is why some speed-reading courses teach readers to read merely the beginnings and endings of paragraphs.

The paragraph break is a big brother to the period: the period divides sentences, while the paragraph break divides groups of sentences. Just as a sentence must have a beginning and appropriate ending, so must a paragraph. Yet while the period is paid homage to as the backbone of punctuation, the paragraph break is largely ignored. This is ironic, since its role could be considered even more pivotal than the period, as it effects not just one sentence, but many. If the period is a stop sign, then the paragraph break is a stoplight at a major intersection.

The section break (also known as the line space) is the most subjective of punctuation marks. It is rarely discussed, and there is not even a consensus on how to indicate it. In manuscript form, this mark is generally indicated by a blank line followed by text set flush left, or by a single asterisk, or by a set of asterisks running across the page, centered and evenly spaced with a tab between each. In a bound book, it is usually indicated by a line space between two paragraphs, but you'll also find it indicated by a wide variety of symbols, from a star, to some small graphic in line with the theme of the book, such as a miniature ship in a book about the sea. Regardless of the visual, they all serve the same purpose: to indicate a section break.

The section break is used to delineate sections within chapters, which might range from several paragraphs to several pages. It signifies a major transition within a chapter, usually a change of time, place, or even viewpoint. It indicates to the reader that, although the chapter isn't finished, he can comfortably pause and digest what he's read. Make no doubt about it: it is a significant break, carrying nearly the weight of a chapter break. The only difference is that the section break defines a transition that, while significant, must fall under the umbrella of a single chapter.

Stronger than a paragraph break yet weaker than a chapter break, it is the semicolon of breaks. It is a big brother to the paragraph break, and a big big brother to the period. If the period is the stop sign and the paragraph break is the stop light, then the section break is the town line.

HOW TO USE PARAGRAPH BREAKS

The chief purpose of a paragraph break is to define and encapsulate a theme. One of the first rules of composition is that every paragraph must have an argument or thesis, must begin with an idea, carry it through, and conclude with it. The opening sentence should set the stage, the middle sentences execute, and the final sentence conclude. A neat, little package. This is easy to do when writing essays or academic papers, but when it comes to fiction or creative nonfiction, you cannot blatantly allow your work to progress so neatly, jumping from argument to argument, without being accused of writing in too linear a fashion, or in an inappropriately academic style. For example, creative writers are told to avoid beginning paragraphs with "thus" or "finally"; the neat building blocks of an academic paper are too linear for the creative world. Which is understandable: readers don't want to feel as if they're progressing from one argument to the next. They want to get caught up in a story.

This leaves the creative writer with a quandary: he must keep his paragraphs focused, yet without appearing to do so. When he opens each paragraph he must subtly suggest a direction, and before its end he must bring it to (or toward) a conclusion. Mastering the paragraph break will help the creative writer in this task. By placing one at just the right moment, a writer can subtly encapsulate a theme and set the stage for a new theme in the paragraph to come.

Let's look at an example from Joyce Carol Oates's story "Heat":

> We went to see them in the funeral parlor where they were waked, we were made to. The twins in twin caskets, white, smooth, gleaming, perfect as plastic, with white satin lining puckered like the inside of a fancy candy box. And the waxy white lilies, and the smell of talcum powder and perfume. The room was crowded, there was only one way in and out.
>
> Rhea and Rhoda were the same girl, they'd wanted it that way.
>
> Only looking from one to the other could you see they were two.

Notice how the first paragraph begins with the image of their entering the funeral parlor; the subsequent sentences expand on this image; and the final sentence concludes with it. When Oates moves on to a new paragraph, she is off describing the parlor and onto a different concept—and none of it is heavy handed. It is subtly suggested by the paragraph break. Note also the terrific contrast between paragraphs here, the impact that the second and third paragraphs have standing on their own as one-sentence paragraphs, especially after coming out of a longer paragraph. This is not haphazard: each sentence reflects the content, hammers home a profound idea.

• Paragraphs are funny things in that they must be both independent and connected. They are like links in a chain, each complete in its own right, yet each attached to another. In order to accomplish this, the opening and closing sentences must inconspicuously act as hooks, propelling us from one paragraph to another. Indeed, the break itself must be thought of as a hook.

There is no comparison between a good paragraph break and a great one. A great one not only encapsulates a theme, but leaves you dangling, *needing* to turn to the next paragraph. Just as the opening and closing of chapters have hooks, so must you take this principle and apply it to the paragraph break. If a paragraph (like a chapter) ends on a note that is too self encapsulated, readers can feel as if they've read enough and not feel compelled to read on. And it must be a two-pronged approach: ending a paragraph with a hook does little good if the following paragraph doesn't, in turn, begin with a strong sentence that ties into the previous ending. Consider the opening lines of F. Scott Fitzgerald's *The Great Gatsby:*

> In my younger and more vulnerable years my father gave me some advice that I've been turning over in my mind ever since.
> "Whenever you feel like criticizing anyone," he told me, "just remember that all the people in this world haven't had the advantages that you've had."

Fitzgerald chooses to begin his novel with two single-sentence paragraphs, a bold move. But it works. It helps to draw the reader in immediately. Notice how each of these paragraphs stands on its own, yet also feels connected to what follows.

• No other punctuation mark rivals the paragraph break when it comes to its power over pacing. Short paragraphs accelerate the pace, while long ones can slow it to a crawl. If your pace is slow, you can increase it with frequent paragraph breaks; if too quick, you can slow it by decreasing their frequency. Of course, this must only be done for a specific reason, not just to arbitrarily speed up or slow down the work. Like all punctuation marks, paragraph breaks can only do so much on their own, and are ultimately at the mercy of the content around them. If you are in the midst of a heated action scene, for instance, frequent breaks might be appropriate—indeed, long paragraphs in an action scene might even be inappropriate. They must conform to the content.

In Ellen Cooney's novel *Gun Ball Hill* the short paragraphs help accelerate the pace at appropriate moments:

> "The English have a genius for prisons," he would tell her.
> They took him at 4:00 in the afternoon. A summer day. August 19.

Note also her use of the period, how the short sentences mimic the short paragraphs, each hammering home a point of significance, each further bringing to life the kidnapping.

Raymond Carver, on the other hand, manages to slow the pace with his short paragraphs in his story "Collectors":

> I was out of work. But any day I expected to hear from up north. I lay on the sofa and listened to the rain. Now and then I'd lift up and look through the curtain for the mailman.
> There was no one on the street, nothing.

Although the paragraphs (and sentences) are short, the pace slows to a crawl. As each point is hammered home, we feel time passing, and nothing happening. Then a new paragraph comes, and still nothing is happening. We are made to feel as the narrator feels.

• The paragraph break is the ultimate balancer. It blocks off a certain size of text, and in doing so wields great power over consistency. For example, a paragraph break can create a one-line paragraph, or a three-page paragraph. If such a paragraph (whether one line or three pages) is thematically encapsulated, then technically the paragraph break fulfills its function. But consistency must be taken into account. One should not have paragraph lengths varying wildly throughout a text. The experience will be too jarring on readers, and they won't be able to settle in.

Thus when inserting a paragraph break, you must also take into account the paragraph breaks that preceded it and those that will follow. The paragraph break, by its nature, is entirely about context (which is why in this chapter we will discuss it here instead of in a separate "context" section). In most cases, you want to set the style by striving for an overall consistency. If your paragraphs average seven sentences, for example, stay as close to that as possible, plus or minus two sentences. This will help establish an overall pace for your book, will help the reader settle in and focus on the content. It will also put you in a position to be able to alert the reader to something important when the time comes.

• Which brings us to breaking with consistency. Once you've offered a general consistency, you can—and should—break the rules, varying paragraph length when the content calls for it. If your work is filled with seven-sentence paragraphs and a one-line paragraph appears, it will hit the reader like a punch; the content in that one-line paragraph will be thrust into the limelight. It's a way of hammering home a point, of indicating extreme significance. Breaking with paragraph length is particularly effective in beginnings and endings, whether of sections, chapters, or the entire book. It can help add a dramatic touch, a feeling of breaking with style, which beginnings and endings often demand.

Here's an exemplary example from Brian Ascalon's Roley novel *American Son:*

Tomas is the son who helps pay the mortgage by selling attack dogs to rich people and celebrities. He is the son who causes her embarrassment by showing up at family parties with his muscles covered in gangster tattoos and his head shaved down to stubble and his eyes bloodshot from pot. He is really half white, half Filipino but dresses like a Mexican, and it troubles our mother that he does this. She cannot understand why if he wants to be something he is not he does not at least try to look white. He is also the son who says that if any girlfriend criticized our mother or treated her wrong he would knock the bitch across the house.

I am the son who is quiet and no trouble, and I help our mother with chores around the house.

By the paragraph break placement alone, we can feel the contrast between the two brothers. The contrast between the two paragraphs is terrific, with the short paragraph truly standing out, hammering home the point that these two brothers couldn't be any more different.

Louise Erdrich uses the paragraph break to great effect in her story "Matchimanito":

I guided the last buffalo hunt. I saw the last bear shot. I trapped the last beaver with a pelt of more than two years' growth. I spoke aloud the words of the government treaty and refused to sign the settlement papers that would take away our woods and lake. I axed the last birch that was older than I, and I saved the last of the Pillager family.

Fleur.

We found her on a cold afternoon in late winter, out in her family's cabin near Matchimanito Lake, where my companion, Edgar Pukwan, of the tribal police, was afraid to go.

Fleur. It is a bold, one-word paragraph, sandwiched between two longer paragraphs; you don't get more conspicuous punctuation than that. And it works. Erdrich signals to us that someone new is on the scene, someone of great significance.

> "Short paragraphs put air around what you write and make it look inviting, whereas one long chunk of type can discourage the reader from even starting to read."
> —WILLIAM ZINSSER

HOW TO USE SECTION BREAKS

When considering whether to use a section break, the first thing you must realize is that every time you use one, you give the reader a chance to put your book down. The section break carries nearly the power of a chapter break and also has nearly the visual appeal of one: it creates a nice, too-convenient place for a reader to rest. So first ask yourself if you truly need it. Can the chapter live without it? If you decide you do need a significant break, then ask yourself if you shouldn't use a chapter break instead. You must have an excellent justification for why these sections must fall under one chapter, instead of being chapters in and of themselves.

If you pass the test of these two questions, then you are ready to use the section break. Sometimes it will be necessary. If so, let's explore some ways to use it:

• Section breaks can indicate a passing of time. While this is more traditionally indicated by a chapter break, there certainly are instances within a chapter where time can pass. For example, you might be dealing with a small amount of time (say, one hour), in which case a section break could be more appropriate than a full-fledged chapter break. Or if your work spans a ten-year period, and each chapter covers one year, and you want to indicate the passing of only a few months, then a section break would be appropriate.

• Section breaks can indicate a change of setting. There might be an instance when you need to change settings within the same chapter; perhaps, for instance, a setting change is a minor one (like going elsewhere within the same town) and thus you'd want a less substantial break. In general, drastic setting changes are better indicated by chapter breaks, particularly if they are coupled with time or viewpoint transitions. What's important is consistency: you don't want to use section breaks to indicate setting changes in one chapter, yet use chapter breaks for the same purpose in subsequent chapters. Whichever route you choose, stick to the course.

• Section breaks can indicate a change in viewpoint. In general, changes in viewpoint should be reserved for chapter breaks; this is among the most substantial of breaks, and readers need time and space to realize they are inside another character's head. The last thing you want to do is switch perspectives within one chapter and have the reader read on, thinking he's still in the original character's point of view; when he finally figures it out, he will have to go back and reread the material, and will be frustrated.

That said, there are rare instances when you might prefer to switch viewpoints within the same chapter. For example, if you have created an ensemble cast and have decided to give each character equal weight and switch viewpoints frequently between them; or if you're dealing with a romance and two characters share equal weight, and you alternate between their viewpoints throughout the work. In such a case, you might alternate viewpoint chapter by chapter, but in the final chapter, when the pace accelerates and they come together, alternate their viewpoints within the very same chapter, in which case you'd use a section break. Even then it would be debatable. If you go this route, it must be justified, and pains must be taken to immediately let readers know that they are in the midst of another viewpoint.

• To indicate transitions where none are indicated. Sometimes you encounter a work where a major transition occurs within a chapter and yet there is nothing to delineate it at all. This will confuse the reader, as he won't realize there has been a change of time, setting, or viewpoint (or some other significant change) until it's too late. He will then have to go back and reread. If a major transition must occur within a chapter, there should usually be a section break. Without it, you leave your work open to confusion.

• Section breaks can offer readers a rest within a long chapter. But keep in mind that needing a rest is not reason enough for a section break. Section breaks should only be used to offer a rest if they *also* meet the criteria of a significant transition. Breaks can't just come for the sake of it—otherwise, readers will pick up exactly where they left off, and wonder why there was a break at all. It devalues the break, and readers won't take it seriously the next time it appears.

If you do end up using a section break, remember that every time you do you create new beginnings and endings. The power of these moments must be taken seriously. Don't use one unless you're prepared to conclude the previous section with a strong hook and begin the new one with an equally strong one. More important, make sure you build to that hook well in advance, and don't just tack it on. Hooks must always be organic to the material, and the best ones take several pages to build.

Let's look at section breaks in literature. Tim O'Brien used it masterfully in his story "The Things They Carried":

> With its quilted liner, the poncho weighed almost two pounds, but it was worth every ounce. In April, for instance, when Ted Lavender was shot, they used his poncho to wrap him up, then to carry him across the paddy, then to lift him into the chopper that took him away.
>
> They were called legs or grunts.

With his punctuation, O'Brien shows us how commonplace death was in Vietnam. In the section's final sentence, discussing common items used by the soldiers, he mentions the poncho, and offhandedly mentions that it can be used to carry away a dead body—as if carrying away a dead body is a routine event. Then he offers a section break, and changes the topic, switching again to something commonplace and reinforcing the idea that a dead body is not worth discussing.

Paul Cody offers one of the most inventive uses of the section break I've seen in the opening of his novel *Compline*:

> 1:00 a.m. Monday, January 6.
>
> Ann left earlier in the evening for Knoxville, where her sister died on Saturday, around 10:00 a.m. After two years with cancer, then a stroke.
>
> Ray is awake, sitting in the dark, sipping wine from a twelve-ounce tumbler.
>
> Outside, the temperature is below zero, and may go down to ten below.

The sky is mostly deep black, with a few scudding clouds. In the backyard, on the other side of the window, a bright half-moon casts the shadows of bare branches on the snow blanketed on the ground.

Ray is staying behind in upstate New York with Eammon and Quentin, their sons, who are ten and seven. The four of them, Ray, Ann, Eammon and Quentin, went to East Tennessee only two weeks ago, when Martha, who had been sick so long, had a massive stroke. They flew down three days before Christmas.

In another author's hands this could be too stylistic, but Cody pulls it off. He begins his novel by hammering home intense images, each a snapshot, a fragment of a scene, pulling us deeper into a dark world. The pauses offered by a section break normally give us a chance to pull away from something dark, to take a break and start something new; but here, Cody shows us that there is no getting away, that even when we take a rest, we will come back to unremitting bleakness.

DANGER OF OVERUSE AND MISUSE OF PARAGRAPH BREAKS

• Overuse. Short paragraphs work well in newspaper and magazine writing, but they are not for the world of books (indeed this problem often plagues journalists-turned-authors). When a reader settles in for three hundred or more pages he expects a consistent pace, and paragraphs define that pace. Readers who turn to books look forward to stretching their attention capacity to absorb seven-sentence paragraphs (or more), and often want to be more mentally challenged than when reading a newspaper article. When paragraph breaks are overused, it creates consistently short paragraphs, which creates a jarring reading experience.

Just as short sentences make for choppy reading, so do short paragraphs. Paragraphs might be conceptualized to be too short to begin with. There is nothing wrong with a short paragraph on occasion, or even a series of them at some pivotal point in the work, but if the work consistently employs short paragraphs, it will be problematic.

• Paragraphs might be too short because they break prematurely, before the direction has a chance to conclude itself. If so, they can usually be fixed by merely moving the break, placing it later, by combining material from the following paragraph. This will fix the symptom, but will not solve the bigger issue: your thought process. Lucid paragraphs, even more than lucid sentences, are the mark of attention span: it takes talent to hold a complex idea in your head during the course of several sentences, to make a paragraph feel like one long thought. Writers with a short attention span will have difficulty in this regard, but even writers with the greatest span will at some point get tired and slip, and end up concluding a paragraph slightly too soon or too late. If so, it indicates you are not thinking as clearly as you should, not conceptualizing paragraphs as a single unit. This means you will also inevitably begin a paragraph on a bad note, since you are beginning with remnant material. Such a work will feel chaotic and will eventually lead a reader to put a work down.

When you conclude a paragraph, you should go back and look at your opening sentence. Have you come full circle? Does more need to be said? Likewise, when you begin a new paragraph, ask yourself if your opening sentence is truly initiating a new idea or if it is merely running on from the previous paragraph. Always ask yourself: Why end here? Why not one sentence earlier, or later? If there is no real answer, readers will feel as if they are in the hands of an arbitrary writer. Nothing can be more lethal.

• Alternately, one encounters works where paragraph breaks don't ever seem to come, where we leave one idea and enter another all under the guise of a single paragraph. This is equally problematic. Without a break, readers will feel as if they're being thrust into a new idea before having a chance to digest the old one. Paragraphs that don't end when they should will also be too long, making it harder for a reader to follow. It is hard enough for a reader to be jolted about by short paragraphs, but with long paragraphs, it is both confusing *and* suffocating.

Again, when you conclude a paragraph, go back and look at your opening sentence. Have you come past full circle? Have you said too much? Always ask yourself: why end here?

Keep in mind, though, that some great authors, like Faulkner and Moody, have underused paragraph breaks deliberately, creating paragraphs that stretch for pages on end. Indeed, in their case, you might even say that the long paragraphs defined their style. Such usage is not verboten, just very stylistic, and should never be attempted without a deliberate reason.

• In the worst case, one encounters paragraphs that have no point or direction at all, that don't begin with a strong idea, don't carry it through, and don't conclude with it. Such paragraphs are so arbitrary that the break becomes completely ineffective, as it is bound to be haphazard no matter where it lands. This is a sure sign of muddled thinking—with paragraphs like these it will be impossible for a work to be concise. For such a writer, the solution will be to focus on the beginnings and endings of paragraphs. When you have a strong beginning it gives you a strong direction; when you have a strong conclusion, you are bound to end up in the right place. With these in place, it is less likely you will ramble in the middle; and if you do, your beginnings and endings will save you, will keep the paragraphs readable enough to keep you on track.

"Punctuation is both an art and a craft; predominately, however, it is an art; a humble art yet far from insignificant art, for it forms a means to an end and is not itself an end. The purpose it serves, the art it subserves, is the art of good writing."

—ERIC PARTRIDGE, *You Have a Point There*

DANGER OF OVERUSE AND MISUSE OF SECTION BREAKS

• Sometimes one encounters a work where there are four, five, or more section breaks per chapter, and the effect is immediate. It lends the chapter a choppy feel, as if it's been carved into small parts. As a rule of thumb, there should rarely be more than one or two section breaks per chapter. There is a certain satisfaction for the reader in absorbing himself in fifteen or twenty pages at once; multiple section breaks detract from that. So many breaks give the reader so many more chances to set your book down. It also makes them work harder, as they'll have to exert the mental energy of going through multiple beginnings and endings, going through major transitions (whether of time, setting, or viewpoint) several times in a single chapter. Such hard work should be reserved for chapter breaks. Frequent section breaks also take away power from the section break itself: readers will trust its impact less if it appears ubiquitously. Section breaks are particularly abrasive in short chapters, in which they should rarely appear.

• Occasionally section breaks are inserted when not truly needed, when a transition is not significant enough. In such cases, the new section will often begin on exactly the same note, with no transition having occurred. The section break becomes arbitrary, and after one or two usages like this, it will lose power.

Section breaks can also be misused as an excuse to abruptly end a scene, which enables a writer to avoid the hard work of developing it. They can become a convenient way for a writer to end on a mysterious, incomplete note, to indicate some greater significance or meaning when in fact there is none. Readers won't skip from section to section very long without realizing there's not much to each of these sections, and will become inclined to set the work down.

• Conversely, sometimes a transition indicated by a section break is too strong, is one that would be best served by a full-fledged chapter break. It can be a fine line deciding whether a section or chapter break is needed, especially as they both indicate significant transitions. Sometimes chapter length will be the determining factor: if every chapter in your work is thirty pages and you are at the fifteen-page mark with a significant transition, for consistency's sake it might be preferable to use the section break. But the solution is not always so clear cut.

If your section breaks are too significant, readers will come to view them in a new way: as chapter breaks. The next time they encounter one, they will anticipate a substantial change and will be more likely to choose this moment to set the book down.

Too-substantial section breaks also take away power from the chapter break: if the section breaks could be chapter breaks in their own right, then what good are chapter breaks? If they can't indicate a break stronger than the section break, chapter breaks become powerless. Chapter breaks serve an important purpose, which is to allow readers to rest, and to digest information.

Too-substantial section breaks also defeat their own purpose: they don't leave readers enough time or breathing room to digest a transition properly; as a result, a major transition (such as change of time, setting, or viewpoint) will be glossed over and won't really sink in.

• Section breaks, like paragraph breaks, are entirely about context; they exist to define a series of paragraphs or pages, to break them into sections and put them in context of the greater chapter. Section breaks themselves must appear in context of the greater work. Thus when deciding whether to insert a section break, you must consider how many section breaks appear, on average, in other chapters throughout your work. For example, if there are four section breaks in chapter one, but none throughout the rest of the work, it will feel inconsistent; or, if every chapter in your work averages one section break and a particular chapter has five, it will feel inconsistent (unless you do this for a deliberate reason). This is a red flag that this chapter doesn't fit in well with the rest, that perhaps it was hurried, or pieced together.

Additionally, you must consider the placement of section breaks within a chapter. A thirty-page chapter with two section breaks might have a break on page ten and a break on page twenty, which would leave you with three ten-page sections. But if the same two breaks were placed on page three and page twenty-six, you would be left with three sections of three pages, twenty-three pages, and four pages, respectively. This could lend a jarring feel. Section breaks needn't always come at precise intervals, but there must be some uniformity—or if you break with uniformity, you must do so for a deliberate reason. The important thing is that you don't do so unknowingly, or haphazardly.

WHAT YOUR USE OF PARAGRAPH AND SECTION BREAKS REVEALS ABOUT YOU

Writers who overuse the paragraph break (creating short paragraphs) are likely to be fast paced, action oriented, and focused on the execution of their plot at any cost—even at the expense of well-crafted prose. They are more likely to be straightforward, functional. They are either beginners, or haven't yet grasped that writing is about the journey. They more likely hail from a journalistic background, where short paragraphs are the norm.

The good news is that these writers are concerned with plot and pacing, that they aim to please the reader, and that they proceed with concise thinking. If they are journalists, their background will serve them well in this regard—but only if they are humble enough to step back and realize that they are now operating in a different medium, and if they are willing to take it on its own terms.

Writers who underuse the paragraph break (creating long paragraphs) fall into two categories: the first, more common, are writers who can't censor themselves. These writers overflow with ideas and blur one into the next. They are less likely to write concisely, and their chapters will also begin and end arbitrarily. Their book as a whole will feel like a mess, and will need much more cutting. Since they don't know how to properly conclude, they are likely to also have a problem with creating effective closing hooks, and their work will likely end several times when it should only end once. They will need to learn how to distinguish thoughts.

The second type of writer crafts long paragraphs that are well thought out, but simply too long. These writers are rare. They will more likely be sophisticated, probably older, and might have an academic or scholarly background. They have a long attention span, are less likely to be action oriented, and are more concerned with prose. This bodes well for the writing itself—style, word choice, execution—but not for plot and pacing. Their work will likely be exceedingly slow, even stylistic. They need to learn that not every reader has the mental capacity that they do, or the desire to exert it.

In all of these cases the writers also misuse the paragraph break, as it is inevitable that too-long or too-short paragraphs will also begin or end on the wrong note. This suggests that they do not think as clearly as they should. This is yet another example where punctuation reveals the writer: messy breaks reveal messy thinking. Clear, lucid breaks reveal clear, lucid thinking. Indeed, we begin to see how punctuation can be used to teach the writer how to think, and subsequently how to write.

Writers who overuse the section break (creating too many sections) are looking for a way out, a stylistic trick to compensate for what they don't offer elsewhere. They are likely to not finish what they started, to leave elements of their work underdeveloped, dangling mysteriously, and not offer the resolution readers crave. They are impatient. These writers think in terms of the individual pieces but not the big picture; indeed, their work will likely feel like a collection of disparate parts.

A book can live happily without section breaks, so it's hard to "underuse" them. That said, there are instances when they could be needed, and in such a case writers who omit them are likely to have little sense of transition. They are less likely to use strong opening or closing hooks, will less likely craft a book that grabs readers. They are less likely to have a flair for drama, and won't have a firm enough grasp on the importance of a switch of time, setting, or viewpoint. As a result, they are likely to not use any of these well.

We must also consider writers who misuse section breaks, which can be a troubling reflection of their thought process. If they insert four section breaks in one chapter and one in another, if they have some sections that run three pages and others that run thirty-three, this can indicate chaotic thought. They are more likely to write in a scattered, uncontrolled way, and their work as a whole will likely lack a defining arc or direction.

EXERCISES

• Examine the final sentences of several of the paragraphs in one of your works, and then go back and reexamine their openings. Are the first and last sentences as related to each other as they should be? Do these paragraphs come full circle? Do any of them end prematurely, or go on too long? Can you edit accordingly? What impact does it have on the work?

• Take two pages from your work and cut the paragraph length in half. You might need to cut or add material so that these paragraphs work at half the length. Take a step back and reread the material. How does it read now? What impact did it have on pacing, on style? Did switching to such a style spark any ideas? Can you apply this technique elsewhere in your work?

• Take two pages from your work and make your paragraphs twice as long. You might need to combine two or more paragraphs, or add new material. Now take a step back and reread the material. How does it read now? What impact did it have on pacing, on style? Did switching to such a style make you feel differently while you were writing? Give you any new ideas? Can you apply this technique elsewhere in your work?

• Take a close look at your paragraph consistency. Count the number of sentences in your paragraphs. Do this for an entire chapter. What is the average? Go back and look at your paragraphs individually and see if any paragraphs significantly exceed or fall short of that length. If so, is there a good reason? If not, can you find a way to balance them out, to shorten or lengthen them to achieve overall consistency? What impact does it have on the work?

• Look through your work for a moment where you'd like to create an impact. To do so, can you contrast a long paragraph with a short one?

• Go back through your work and ask yourself if any of your chapters (particularly long chapters) contain significant transitions, for example, transitions in time, setting, or viewpoint. Can a section break be inserted at any of these moments to help mark the transition?

• Take a close look at the material that immediately precedes and follows your section breaks. Are there strong opening and closing hooks? If not, can you strengthen them?

• Take a close look at your section breaks and ask yourself if you use any of them as an easy way out, as a way of avoiding diving deeper into a character or scene. Can you expand the material before the section break? (When you're finished, you might find that the section break is no longer even necessary.)

• Take a close look at your section breaks and ask if any of these are *too* significant. Should any of them be replaced with full-fledged chapter breaks?

• You can learn a lot about section breaks by studying how poets use stanza breaks. Read through a wide variety of poetry, looking specifically for these breaks. When are the poets using stanza breaks? What does it add to the poem? What can this teach you about section breaks? How might this principle be applied to your own writing?

Part 3

PROCEED
WITH
CAUTION

THE QUESTION MARK, EXCLAMATION POINT, ITALICS, POINTS OF ELLIPSIS, AND THE HYPHEN

My attitude toward punctuation is that it ought to be as conventional as possible. The game of golf would lose a good deal if croquet mallets and billiard cues were allowed on the putting green. You ought to be able to show that you can do it a good deal better than anyone else with the regular tools before you have a license to bring in your own improvements.

—ERNEST HEMINGWAY

I RECEIVED hundreds of letters in response to my first book on writing, *The First Five Pages*. Many readers loved the book, some hated it, and others told me with a dark satisfaction that they didn't read past *my* first five pages. Accustomed to receiving thousands of query letters a year, some truly bizarre, none of this really surprised me.

What did surprise me was the number of readers who wrote asking me to elaborate on what I'd said about the question mark. I had touched on the subject of punctuation briefly in *The First Five Pages*, devoting a mere two pages to it. Within those two pages were a mere three sentences devoted to the question mark. But for some reason readers fixated on these three sentences.

In this final chapter I will fully address the usage of the question mark, along with other punctuation marks that should be used sparingly, or not at all, in creative writing.

USE SPARINGLY

The Question Mark

There is nothing wrong with the question mark in its own right. It is a perfectly fine punctuation mark, and even necessary in many cases. Obviously, it serves a purpose that no other punctuation mark can: to indicate a question. It can also be used creatively to capture a certain form of dialogue, where the character speaks with a rising inflection. This is often found in casual speech, where the speaker is stating a fact yet also trying to discern whether his listener is listening (or understanding). For example:

"I was walking to the store? You know, the one on 8th street?"

That said, you must remember that a publishing professional is looking to reject a manuscript as quickly as he can. This entails scrutinizing the first five pages, particularly the first page. And an abundance of question marks in the first pages—particularly in the first paragraph—nearly always indicate amateur or melodramatic writing. For some reason, the poor question mark gets seized upon by the writer who is desperate to immediately hook the reader in a cheap way. For example, I have seen too many opening lines like this:

Did I kill my wife?

Or:

Did I think I'd get away with it?

Or:

Did she really do it?

It feels gimmicky, and actually distances a reader more than entraps him. These writers don't realize that readers, when beginning a book, are prepared to make a mental effort; they don't need to be treated as if they'll put the book down if they don't like the first sentence. It is overkill.

Never use the question mark to create drama. Let it fulfill its role organically, when (or if) it needs to. Always ask yourself if a sentence can somehow be paraphrased. For example, some "questions" might be indicated with periods:

"You didn't really think you'd get away with it?"

Could also be:

"You didn't really think you'd get away with it."

The latter is more subtle, indicating a flat intonation; it is more of a statement than a question. Always consider the desired inflection of the speaker.

Also realize that there is less license for the question mark in creative writing. Practical nonfiction and self-help books can get away with it more easily, particularly if they are prescriptive or directly questioning the reader, for example in an exercise section.

The Exclamation Point
So many people have beaten up on the poor exclamation point (including myself) that I feel bad delivering it yet one more punch. The exclamation point has been referred to as "the period that blew its top," is known as a "screamer" by journalists. Harry Shaw says,

"Unless you wish your writing to seem juvenile or empty-headed, follow this rule: Never use an exclamation point when another mark will serve adequately and properly." F. Scott Fitzgerald says "an exclamation mark is like laughing at your own joke." Clearly, the exclamation point has many enemies.

Thus let me begin by being contrary: like the question mark, the exclamation point does have its place, does fulfill a role that no other punctuation mark can. There are times when it will be useful, even necessary. For example, to indicate a direct command:

Stop!

Or to indicate someone shouting:

Wait for me!

Or to indicate extreme surprise:

I can't believe it!

Which, by the way, can also be done in conjunction with the question mark (although this usage is debatable):

You mean her!?

To indicate extreme pain:

Ouch!

Or anger:

You son of a bitch!

Or any other extreme emotion. Indeed, *extreme* is the exclamation point's modus operandi.

This said, the reason so many attack the exclamation point is because, like the question mark, it can be painfully misused. Like the question mark, it can be used as a crutch to create a heightened sense of drama, can be transformed into a screaming car salesman. As a rule, if you need an exclamation point to make a scene come alive, then you better reexamine that scene. Drama should always be built naturally and organically, and not need a ploy to grab a reader's attention.

Ultimately, the problem with the exclamation point is that it's too powerful, too attention grabbing. It's the bright green dress, the flaming pink scarf. There may be an occasion, once every five years, when it is needed; until then, like those clothes, it is best left in the closet.

> "It is a sound principle that as few stops should be used as will do the work."
> —H. W. AND F. G. FOWLER, *The King's English*

Italics

Italics are a graceful form of punctuation, and in emphasizing a word or phrase they fulfill a role no other punctuation mark can. There are instances when they are needed. If a sentence is open to interpretation, italics can clarify, provide emphasis to a particular word in order to let readers know how to read it. For example:

He was angry that I didn't pick up the phone, but it was *his* mother and I didn't see why I should have to.

Or they can contrast two words in a sentence:

You might like it but *she* hates it.

They can also be used to indicate thought, to contrast a narrator's interior monologue with the exterior world:

My father's friend grabbed my hand.
"Nice to meet you!" he said.
What a snake.
"Nice to meet you, too," I answered, despite myself.

The problem, though, with italics is that writers can easily become addicted, and allow themselves to believe they are needed everywhere. For example:

His exam was *three* hours long. He *never* expected it to be so *hard,* and now he had second doubts over whether he was *truly* prepared.

At first glance the italics may seem necessary, but if you remove them you'll find that the sentence is equally understood without them:

His exam was three hours long. He never expected it to be so hard, and now he had second doubts over whether he was truly prepared.

Readers might not grasp the emphasis as quickly, but eventually they will—and allowing the reader that satisfaction is always preferable. If stresses and meanings are too laid out, if you tell readers at every step how to read your book, they will grow to resent you for underestimating them.

Italics are also annoying because whenever they appear, it is the writer's voice appearing, telling the reader how he, the writer, would emphasize the sentence. It can be overbearing. Like the question mark and exclamation point, italics are a strong visual, and wield tremendous power. They can dominate a text without even trying. And they can also defeat their own purpose: italics overused quickly lose their power, and have little import the next time they appear. From a publishing professional's perspective, an overitalicized work is a sure sign of an unrestrained writer.

Finally, italics are, on some level, an admission of failure: every time you use one, you concede that you are unable to construct a sentence in a way that naturally emphasizes stress. This is why the Fowler brothers call italics "a confession of weakness."

Points of Ellipsis
Like the other marks in this section, there is nothing inherently wrong with the ellipsis, and it does have its place. It performs a unique function in allowing a writer to indicate a trailing off, or a brief passing of time. It is at its most restrained, and most effective, within dialogue:

> The doctor approached her gravely, and put a hand on her shoulder. He said, "Your friend . . . might not live."

In an amateur's hands, though, ellipsis points can be a problem. Like italics, they can become a bad habit, a crutch to use whenever a writer doesn't know how to firmly end a sentence or section or chapter, when he doesn't know how to indicate a passing of time any other way. Worst of all, it can become a cheap device to end sections or chapters; some writers think that merely because they conclude with (. . .) it will force the reader to read on. This is silly. A reader doesn't turn a page because of three dots; he turns a page because of content.

Thus it is not surprising that these three dots are almost always used as a ploy, tacked onto an ending that has no dramatic merit in its own right. It's like shouting "Stay tuned!" It brings to mind the gimmicky endings of *Batman*, the television series, in which the characters are put into a dire situation as a cheap trick to make viewers tune in the following week.

Hyphen

The hyphen has a limited creative use in connecting two words into a compound word. Poets regularly use it for this function; indeed, by connecting unlikely words, you can nearly create your own language. Be sparing in doing so, though; it is attention grabbing. Some writers overdo wordplay, creating a witty vocabulary of their own, but at the expense of distracting from the narrative.

More importantly, be careful not to confuse the hyphen with a dash. These are two separate creatures. The hyphen is indicated by a single horizontal line (-) while the dash must be indicated by two typed hyphens, which connect to form one longer horizontal line, sometimes indicated like this (--) and sometimes like this (—). Either one is acceptable when indicating a dash, but the hyphen (-) definitely is not.

DON'T USE AT ALL

There are certain punctuation marks that have no place at all in creative writing. I have no idea why they keep appearing, and assume they are simply confused with other marks. So let's clarify this once and for all:

Brackets

These should never be used in creative writing. They have a limited technical use (mainly to indicate omitted or substituted words in a quotation), but in creative writing they have no place. The only reason I even bring them up is because occasionally you see them confused with parentheses. Make no doubt about it: these are entirely different creatures, not even fourth cousins. (By the way, the British call our parentheses "brackets," so don't confuse the two.)

Underline

It is questionable to even consider this a punctuation mark: some writers do, others don't. Back when typewriters ruled the world, the norm was to underline text in order to indicate to the printer that such text would ultimately need to be italicized. Now, with computers, we can italicize text ourselves. Underlining is a thing of the past, and should not be used.

Bold

This is not truly a punctuation mark, but it is worth mentioning here. If italics and underlining are included in most discussions of punctuation, then the use of boldface should be, too. The reason it's worth mentioning is because when writers are desperate to make something stand out, they'll try every trick there is—ALL CAPS, underline, italics, and even bold. I can't tell you how many query letters I've received sprinkled with bold, and how many times this spilled over into the manuscript itself. Bold should never be used. Emphasis can be indicated with italics, or, when referring to a title in a query letter, in ALL CAPS—but never bold. The only time bold might be used is in a practical work of nonfiction, but even then, only for chapter or header titles, and never in the text itself.

THE SYMPHONY OF
PUNCTUATION

Punctuation is ruled two-thirds by rule and one-third by personal taste.

—G. V. CAREY,
Mind the Stop

THE WORLD of punctuation is a complex one, each mark having its own needs and rules. Sometimes marks will complement one another, at other times they will be in conflict. A period won't feel the same when preceded by a semicolon. A comma won't do as well near a dash. A colon won't allow a semicolon in the same sentence. Quotation marks need paragraph breaks in order to shine. And the slightest change to any of these marks will reverberate throughout the work, affecting sentence, paragraph, section, and chapter. Punctuation marks are skittish. A rock isn't needed for a ripple effect—a pebble is.

Grasping how to use a mark in its own right is difficult enough; mastering how to use it in context of the content, and in context of all the other punctuation marks, is a lifelong endeavor. It is truly an art. But it is worth the effort. When we look at punctuation collectively, we begin to see that punctuation marks, in the right hands, can truly bring out the best in one another. A period used with a dash becomes so much more than a period on its own could ever be. We begin to see that punctuation marks by themselves are like colors in a palette: it is only through the collective that they become all they were meant to be.

But this is abstract. In order to better understand the symphony of punctuation, let's look at what the masters have done over centuries. We return to E. M. Forster's brilliant novel *A Passage to India*:

> Houses do fall, people are drowned and left rotting, but the general outline of the town persists, swelling here, shrinking there, like some low but indestructible form of life.
>
> Inland, the prospect alters.

In the first sentence, Forster uses commas to capture the feeling of a town ebbing and flowing; he also gives us a long sentence, asking us to take it all in at once. He follows this with a paragraph break and a short sentence, which allows the next sentence to provide a sharp contrast. This furthers the purpose of his content, showing the contrast between his two settings. Best of all, he is subtle: the punctuation weaves itself seamlessly through the text, might even be missed if you were not looking for it.

Here's an example from Henry James's "The Tree of Knowledge":

> Such a triumph had its honour even for a man of other triumphs—a man who had reached fifty, who had escaped marriage, who had lived within his means, who had been in love with Mrs. Mallow for years without breathing it, and who, last but not least, had judged himself once for all.

Notice how he avoids commas in the first portion of the sentence, which allows us to rush headlong into a dash, which in turn sets us up for a grand summary, an elaboration. That elaboration is carried out with an abundance of commas, which breaks up the style of the sentence and helps contrast the second portion of the sentence to the first. The commas also mimic items in a list, subtly hinting that we should take with a grain of salt what the character considers "triumphs."

Vladimir Nabokov adroitly uses punctuation in his story "Signs and Symbols":

> For the fourth time in as many years they were confronted with the problem of what birthday present to bring a young man who was incurably deranged in his mind. He had no desires. Manmade objects were to him either hives of evil, vibrant with a malignant activity that he alone could perceive, or gross comforts for which no use could be found in his abstract world. After eliminating a number of articles that might offend him or frighten him (anything in the gadget line for instance was taboo), his parents chose a dainty and innocent trifle: a basket with ten different fruit jellies in ten little jars.

He begins with a long sentence, devoid of commas. He follows with a short sentence, which provides a nice contrast for the first and third sentences. In the third sentence he brings in commas, and in the final sentence he brings in parentheses and then even a colon, allowing for first a building effect and then a wonderful feeling of finality. Even the paragraph break is well timed: he opens the paragraph with a problem and breaks it having resolved that problem.

Let's look at an example from Edith Wharton's story "The Muse's Tragedy":

> Danyers afterwards liked to fancy that he had recognized Mrs. Anerton at once; but that, of course, was absurd, since he had seen no portrait of her—she affected a strict anonymity, refusing even her photograph to the most privileged—and from Mrs. Memorall, whom he revered and cultivated as her friend, he had

extracted but the one impressionist phrase: "Oh, well, she's like one of those old prints where the lines have the value of color."

Using varied punctuation, Wharton manages to prolong a sentence that would otherwise be too long. Calling on the semicolon, double dash, colon, comma, and quotation marks in a single sentence (!) she creates enough ebbs and flows to allow such a length. Notice also her unusual placement of quotation marks at the conclusion; it makes us feel as if the quotation is inherently connected to what came before.

Cynthia Ozick also varies her punctuation in her story "The Shawl":

> Rosa did not feel hunger; she felt light, not like someone walking but like someone in a faint, in trance, arrested in a fit, someone who is already a floating angel, alert and seeing everything, but in the air, not there, not touching the road. As if teetering on the tips of her fingernails.

Notice her immediate use of the semicolon, which offsets the idea that she did not feel hunger, and sets it up to be contrasted to what follows. She then switches to abundant commas, which capture the feeling of the content, evokes what it's like to feel "light," each comma buoying us further up in the air. Finally, she concludes with a short sentence and immediate period; this is conspicuous, since the final sentence could have easily been tacked on to the previous sentence with a comma, and it helps once again to provide contrast, and to emphasize the notion that she felt as if she were "teetering."

Consider this example from Jack London's "In a Far Country":

> How slowly they grew! No; not so slowly. There was a new one, and there another. Two—three—four; they were coming too fast

to count. There were two growing together. And there, a third had joined them. Why, there were no more spots. They had run together and formed a sheet.

This comes toward the conclusion of the story, when the character is freezing to death, hallucinating and envisioning icicles surrounding him. The punctuation helps capture this feeling. First, it is hysterical and chaotic: we have an exclamation point; we have a semicolon coming after the very first word in a sentence; we have two solo dashes following each other; another immediate semicolon; and a series of short, abrupt sentences. All these marks work together to capture his demise.

Perhaps no story better illustrates this principle than Edgar Allan Poe's "The Tell-Tale Heart." Consider the incredibly bold opening line:

> True!—nervous—very, very dreadfully nervous I had been and am; but why *will* you say that I am mad?

We find an exclamation point after the very first word, followed by a dash, followed by another dash after a single word, followed by a conspicuous comma to repeat the word "very," followed by a semicolon, an italicized word, and finally a question mark. Poe achieves it all in the first sentence: we already know that we can't trust this narrator. The punctuation says it all.

Poets tend to be skillful at balancing a symphony of punctuation; their medium allows them to hold an entire work in their head at once, and thus they can get a better overview of the punctuation as a whole. They also need to call on as much varied punctuation as they can, given their finite space. Consider this excerpt from Daniel Halpern's poem "Summer, 1970":

Your black hair a wood scent and dark,
the thickness of pitch or dark amber—
an olfaction of night. We go inside
to comb your hair. You bring brandy, there is glass
on wood, our tongues on fire, the flames licking
the lonely caves of speech by day, together
here, moving quickly in silence.

He begins by being spare with commas and adding a conspicuous dash. Then he follows with a short sentence. Thus far, it is a halting feeling. But once they get inside, he offers a long sentence, filled with commas, which evokes the feeling of letting it all out.

My left eye is blind and jogs like
a milky sparrow in its socket;
my nose is large and never flares
in anger, the front teeth, bucked,
but not in lechery—I sucked
my thumb until the age of twelve.

This comes from Jim Harrison's poem "Sketch for a Job Application Bank." He begins with no commas, allowing the clause to rush into a semicolon; he follows with several commas, then switches to a dash, enabling him to change direction. The punctuation here lets him describe his features in one long sweep, yet also allows the reader a pause for emphasis when need be. Note also the placement of line breaks: "flares" is made to stand out, as is "bucked" and "sucked" (which also rhyme); these breaks unconsciously help signal images he'd like to emphasize.

"The art of punctuation is of infinite consequence in writing; as it contributes to the perspicuity, and consequently to the beauty, of every composition."
—JOSEPH ROBERTSON,
"An Essay on Punctuation," 1785

As if all of this were not tricky enough, complicating matters, you will always find great writers who break the rules, who defy every convention of punctuation and yet still somehow manage to come off better for it. Consider, for example, this excerpt from Kent Meyers's novel *The River Warren*:

> Prayers, that's what it was. I been living across from that house for twenty-two years, and I seen some odd things go on there, I'll admit I like to stand and watch.

By all convention, there should be some other mark before "I'll admit," such as a period, dash, parentheses, colon, or even semicolon. A comma is the most unlikely choice, and at first is jarring. But upon reflection, you come to see that it actually works for the voice of the character. Consider this example from Donald Rawley's "The Bible of Insects":

> These are the women Inez knows she will never be. They are twenty-four and blond, in billowing beige chiffon, standing in open doorways of their grandfathers' houses. They are used to massive walls of stone, crystal, candlelight, and the smug silence of being better. Inez never had, and never will have, that Grace Kelly chignon, that Elizabeth Taylor white dress, that Joan Fontaine way of craning one's neck so attractively.

Again, by all convention there should be a colon or dash in the opening line after "never be." But Rawley, one of the great stylists, instead chooses a period. It is a subtle, unusual approach. Edgar Allan Poe also defies convention in his story "The Unparalleled Adventure of One Hans Pfaall":

> Nevertheless, about noon, a slight but remarkable agitation became apparent in the assembly: the clattering of ten thousand tongues succeeded; and, in an instant afterward, ten thousand faces were upturned toward the heavens, ten thousand pipes descended simultaneously from the corners of ten thousand mouths, and a shout, which could be compared to nothing but the roaring of Niagara, resounded long, loudly, and furiously, through all the city and through all the environs of Rotterdam.

The semicolon coming on the heels of the colon here is unusual indeed. Most writers would have opted for a period instead. While it is not necessarily "correct," it is by no means incorrect either. Some will like it, others won't, but in either case, it helps define Poe's particular style.

It seems there is as much to unlearn from the great writers as there is to learn. James Joyce disliked the quotation mark, and opted for dashes instead. E. E. Cummings disliked capital letters and printed everything in lowercase. Emily Dickinson used an abundance of dashes. George Bernard Shaw used an abundance of colons; Virginia Woolf, an abundance of semicolons. Melville used semicolons questionably. Gertrude Stein and Cormac McCarthy avoided commas. And Shakespeare did anything he wanted.

What can we take away from all of this? It is important to break the rules, especially when they can be as nebulous as they are in the punctuation world. Indeed, breaking the rules will enable breakthroughs in your writing, in your voice, your style, rhythm, viewpoint. Experiment as much as you can. But at the end of the day, only keep what works for the text, what best reflects the content. Breaking the rules only works when a writer has great respect for the rules he breaks.

By this point in the book, if you've applied yourself and worked with the exercises, you will have a good handle on the marks of punctuation a creative writer needs. Now the work begins. Now you must see if you can make them all work together in one grand symphony of punctuation. It is time to put your knowledge to the test, and take a giant, first step into the world of punctuation.

As you do, remember to keep in mind two important principles. The first is that there is great merit to punctuating scarcely, only when you absolutely must. Just as word economy should be strived for, so should punctuation economy.

The second is to let your punctuation unfold organically, as the text demands. Punctuation should never be forced on a text, never be brought in to rescue you from confusing sentence construction. It is not here to save — it is here to complement. This is an important distinction. The sentence itself must do the work. If it does, the punctuation will coexist seamlessly, and you will never have an awkward struggle to squeeze in a dash, or make a semicolon work. If you find yourself having such a struggle, reexamine your sentence structure, your word choice. More likely than not, you will need to rewrite, not repunctuate. As we have seen many times throughout this book, in the best writing the punctuation is seamless, invisible, at one with the text. It will never stand out. You know you are punctuating the best you possibly can when, ironically, you don't even know it's there.

Punctuating masterfully is an ongoing struggle, and the destination will always be somewhere off on the horizon. But it is a journey worthwhile. If you cultivate awareness and are willing to learn, punctuation will perpetually teach you something new about yourself. As we learned throughout the book, punctuation reveals the writer, and revelation is the first step toward self-awareness. If you are willing to listen to what the page is telling you about yourself, and humble enough to change, you will become a better writer.

Punctuation is here to point the way.

SUGGESTED READING

You Have a Point There by Eric Partridge
Writing with Style by John R. Trimble
The Associated Press Guide to Punctuation by Rene J. Cappon
The King's English by H. W. and F. G. Fowler
Punctuate It Right! by Harry Shaw
Eats, Shoots & Leaves by Lynne Truss
Write Right! by Jan Venolia

ABOUT THE AUTHOR

NOAH LUKEMAN is author of the bestselling *The First Five Pages: A Writer's Guide to Staying Out of the Rejection Pile* (Simon & Schuster, 1999), already part of the curriculum in many universities. He is also author of the bestselling *The Plot Thickens: 8 Ways to Bring Fiction to Life* (St. Martin's Press, 2002), a BookSense 76 Selection, a *Publishers Weekly* Daily pick, and a selection of the Writers Digest Book Club. He has also worked as a collaborator, and is coauthor, with Lieutenant General Michael "Rifle" DeLong, USMC, Ret., of *Inside CentCom: The Unvarnished Truth About the Wars in Afghanistan and Iraq* (Regnery, 2004), a Main Selection of the Military Book Club. He has contributed to *Poets & Writers, Writers Digest, The Writer*, and to *The Writers Market*, and was anthologized in *The Practical Writer* (Penguin, 2004). His books have been published in the UK, and foreign editions have been published in Portuguese, Japanese, Korean, Chinese, and Indonesian.

Noah Lukeman is also president of Lukeman Literary Management Ltd, a New York–based literary agency, which he founded in 1996. His clients include winners of the Pulitzer Prize, American Book Award, Pushcart Prize, and O. Henry Award, finalists for the National Book Award, Edgar Award, Pacific Rim Prize, multiple *New York Times* bestsellers, national journalists, major celebrities, and faculty of universities ranging from Harvard to Stanford. He has worked as a manager in the New York office of Artists Management Group, Michael Ovitz's multitalent management company, and has worked for another New York literary agency. Prior to becoming an agent he worked on the editorial side of several major publishers, including William Morrow and Farrar, Straus & Giroux, and as editor of a literary magazine.

He has been a guest speaker on the subjects of writing and publishing at numerous forums, including the Wallace Stegner writing program at Stanford University and the Writers Digest Conference at BookExpo America. He earned his B.A. with High Honors in English and Creative Writing from Brandeis University, cum laude.

To contact the author or comment about this book, visit
www.adashofstyle.com